FABRIC ARCHITECTURE

FABRIC ARCHITECTURE

CREATIVE RESOURCES FOR SHADE, SIGNAGE, AND SHELTER

SAMUEL J. ARMIJOS

W. W. Norton & Company

New York • London

Copyright © 2008 by Samuel J. Armijos

All rights reserved
Printed in China
First Edition

For information about permission to reproduce selections from this book, write to
Permissions, W. W. Norton & Company, Inc., 500 Fifth Avenue, New York, NY 10110

For information about special discounts for bulk purchases, please contact
W. W. Norton Special Sales at specialsales@wwnorton.com or 800-233-4830

Manufacturing by Colorprint Offset
Book design by Jonathan D. Lippincott
Production Manager: Leeann Graham

Library of Congress Cataloging-in-Publication Data
Armijos, Samuel J.
 Fabric architecture / Samuel Armijos. — 1st ed.
  p. cm.
 Includes bibliographical references and index.
 ISBN 978-0-393-73236-8 (hardcover)
 1. Roofs, Fabric. 2. Tents. 3. Tensile architecture. I. Title.
 TH2449.A76 2008
 721'.04498—dc22
          2007030009

ISBN 13: 978-0-393-73236-8

W. W. Norton & Company, Inc., 500 Fifth Avenue, New York, N.Y. 10110
www.wwnorton.com

W. W. Norton & Company Ltd., Castle House, 75/76 Wells Street, London W1T 3QT

0 9 8 7 6 5 4 3 2 1

Page 2: See page 17.
Page 256: Arch-supported membrane roof structure, British Racing Drivers Club, Silverston, United Kingdom. Architen Landrell
Page 260: Clarke Quay shopping mall, view from below. Allsop Architects. Hightexworld
Page 262: Textile Façade exterior shading system, Mesa Arts Center, Mesa, Arizona. Architects: BOORA Architects, FTL Design Engineering Studio, FabriTec Structures
Page 268: Tubaloon Performance Shelter, Konsberg, Norway. Architects: SNØHETTA. Canobbio
Page 270: Celebration Park Pavilion, Allen, Texas. Architects: Clark Condon Associates, FabriTec Structures
Page 271: Bale ring detail, Las Vegas Premium Outlet Mall, Las Vegas, Nevada. Architect: Adams Hennon Group with FTL Design Engineering Studio. FabriTec Structures
Page 272: Stratford Bus Interchange at night, Stratford, London, United Kingdom. Architen Landrell

This book is dedicated to my wife, Miriam, my children, Jay Samuel and Kay Clara, and my parents, Samuel and Esmeralda Armijos.

ACKNOWLEDGMENTS

Special thanks to:

USA Shade and Fabric Structures
Fabritec Structures
Shade Structures
Sunports
Vehicle Protection Structures

Thanks also to the following, who have supported, inspired, and contributed to my passion:

Anchor Industries
Joe Belli
Horst Berger, PE
Nigel Browne
Geoffrey Bruce
David Campbell, PE
Federico Canobbio
John M. Carter
David Chen, PE
Claude Centner
Garry Crowell, FAIA
Todd Dalland, FAIA
Joseph DeNardis, PE
Bart Dreiling
Debra Drew
Benoit Fauchon
François Fournier
Steve Fredrickson
Donald Friedman, PE
Nicholas Goldsmith, FAIA
Nancy Green

Chris Griffin
Pat Hayes
Alex Heslop, RIBA
Kristen Holt-Browning
D.H. Hwang
Tom Kelmartin, PE
Klaus Michael Koch
Natta Ravi Kumar
Mal McLaren, PE
Mark and Darlene Miller
Bill Moss
Jerry O'Connell
Frei Otto
Paul Petizian
Jon Pudenz
Wayne Rendely, PE
Jairo Rios
Debra Roth
Brian Rowinski
Craig Schwitter, PE
Rocky Sconda

Ashish Soni
Dr. William Spillers, PE
Gisela Stromeyer
M. Ali Tayar
Cindy Thompson
David Wakefield, PE
Martin Weigel
Gerry and Suzanne Warner
Bruce Wright, AIA

CONTENTS

INTRODUCTION   11

NOTE ON THE PHOTOGRAPHS   25

1: AWNINGS AND CANOPIES   27

2: UMBRELLAS   49

3: INTERIOR APPLICATIONS   69

4: TENTS AND TEMPORARY STRUCTURES   93

5: SHADE STRUCTURES   121

6: TEXTILE FAÇADES   141

7: MAST-SUPPORTED STRUCTURES   153

8: ARCH- AND FRAME-SUPPORTED STRUCTURES   181

9: POINT-SUPPORTED STRUCTURES   213

10: FUTURE STRUCTURES   235

RESOURCES   257

BIBLIOGRAPHY   261

INDEX   263

ABOUT THE SAMPLES   269

IN-1. Las Vegas Premium Outlet Mall at night, Las Vegas, Nevada. Adams Hennon Architects. Fabritec Structures

INTRODUCTION

Fabric structures are among the oldest forms of architecture, dating back to nomadic times, when shelters were made of animal skins and tree branches. Throughout history, they have been adapted in one form or another by different groups of people living in a variety of environmental conditions. These structures have evolved over the years with advances in materials and technology, and are growing in importance today.

Architectural fabric structures—also referred to as tensile membrane structures, textile buildings, or fabric roofs, to mention just a few terms—come in a variety of shapes and sizes (IN-1). They can be inside, outside, permanent, temporary, large, small, air-supported, air-inflated, tensioned, or draped. These unique forms have played a major role in modern architecture, interior design, and special events since tensile structures were introduced to the world by the noted German architect and engineer Frei Otto (1925–).

The term "fabric" refers to the material or membrane used to create these lightweight structures. The material may have an open weave or be constructed of woven base cloths of varying strengths, and it is protected by a coating to provide thermal, fire, water, and ultraviolet (UV)-light resistance and protection from the elements. Today's fabric structures are designed and constructed independent of geography. They transform space and have both a festive and an elegant quality. Fabric structures are used for a variety of purposes. Besides providing temporary housing for garden parties, circuses, and disaster victims, they serve as amphitheaters, sports stadiums, airports, atriums, building facades, interiors for special events, festive pavilions for housing, parks, resorts, and more.

The term "fabric architecture" encompasses not only sophisticated tensioned membrane structures, but also beautiful forms of sculpture, visual display, signage, and shelters made with modern fabrics that can be erected quickly anywhere in the world, either temporarily or permanently. Seeing one of these structures, a viewer might be tempted to think they are nothing but steel, fabric, and cables, but they are not as easy to construct as they look. Architectural fabric structures require a unique collaboration among designers, engineers, manufacturers, fabricators, and installers. The size and extent of the team depends on the complexity of the project.

Fabric Architecture is intended to educate those interested in designing and building fabric structures, from novices to professionals. It is not a technical book, but rather a treasury of images ranging from interior stretch fabric sculpture to tents and awnings, dome stadiums, and unique lightweight structures using durable architectural fabrics and films. It is not focused on engineering matters or historical perspective, but rather on aesthetic and creative issues. It is intended to inspire, and to help you make your fabric structure a reality. To learn more about the history of fabric structures or their technical aspects, see Frei Otto's *Complete Works*, Horst Berger's *Light Structures: Structures of Light*, Klaus-Michael Koch's *Membrane Structures*, and Tensinet's *European Design Guide for Tensile Surface Structures*, all listed in the Bibliography.

DESIGNING ARCHITECTURAL FABRIC STRUCTURES: A BRIEF OVERVIEW

Designing even simple fabric structures so that they hold up under a variety of conditions can be a complex task. Each component is both visible and structural, and relies on all parts to function properly.

The first step in designing a fabric structure is to create a form with sufficient pre-stress or tension to prevent it from fluttering like a flag or sail (IN-2). Lightweight structures with minimal surfaces optimally should have double curvature, a surface that possesses a high-point (positive) curvature along one principal axis and a low-point (negative) curvature along the other principal axis. *Anticlastic* surface forms have double curvature in diametrically opposite directions, like a saddle, while *synclastic* surface forms have double curvature in the same direction, like a balloon. The degree of curvature depends upon the type and weave of the fabric as well as the type and direction of the loads. The three basic forms associated with tensioned fabric structures are the hypar (hyperbolic paraboloid), the cone, and the barrel vault. The hypar, or simple saddle, is often a square or rectangular form in plan that in elevation is a series of high and low

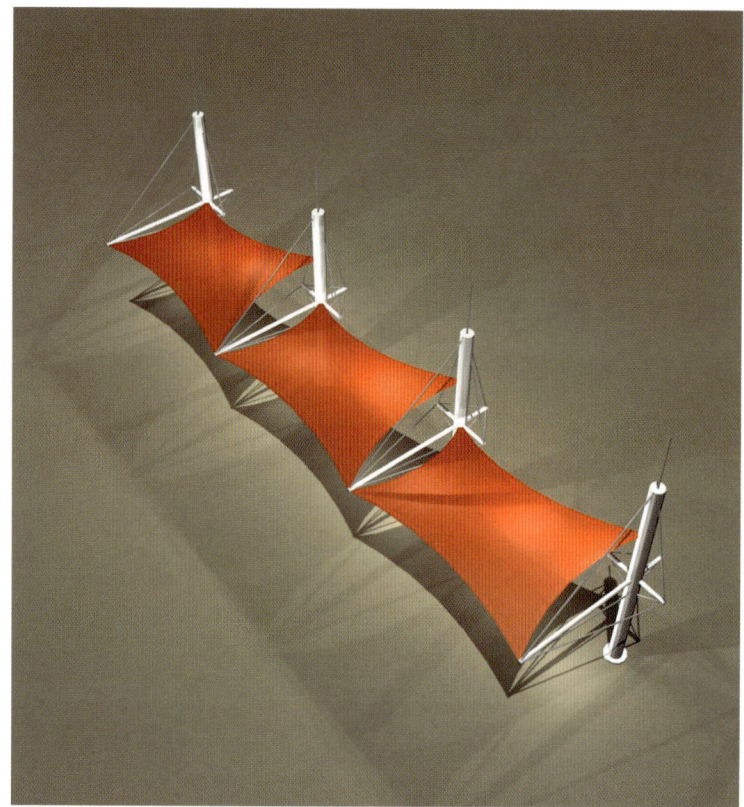

IN-2. Sail structure concept rendering, Long Branch, New Jersey. Fabritec Structures

points (IN-2a). Mast- and point-supported structures are cone forms (IN-2b). Arch- and frame-supported structures, in which the membrane is supported by a compression member, are barrel vaults (IN-2c).

The second step of the design process is to determine the boundaries of the tensioned fabric (IN-3). Boundaries include frames, walls, beams, columns, and anchor points. The fabric is either continuously clamped to frames, walls, or beams or attached to columns and anchor points with membrane plates with adjustable tensioning hardware. Membrane plates are custom designed plates used to link the membrane and edge cables to the structural supports [see IN-20]. In most cases the fabric forms a curved edge or catenary between connection points, requiring a cable, webbing belt, or rope to carry loads to the major structural points. "Catenary" describes the scalloped edge shape of the boundary of a uniformly stressed fabric structure attached only at specific end points or nodes. Catenaries

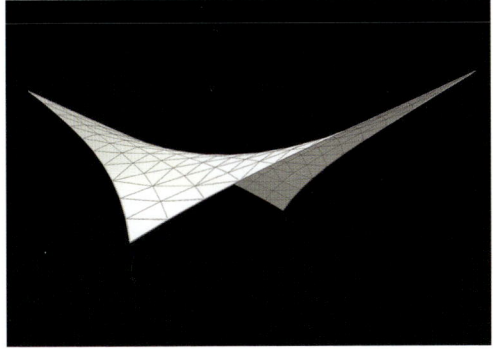
IN-2a. Hypar form.

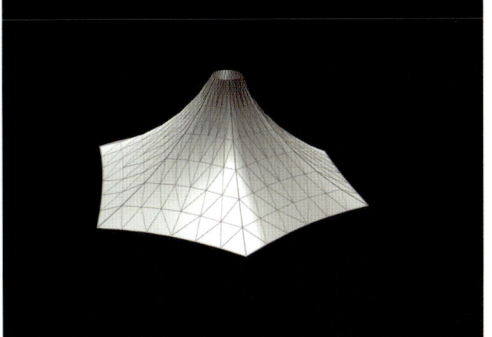
IN-2b. Cone form.

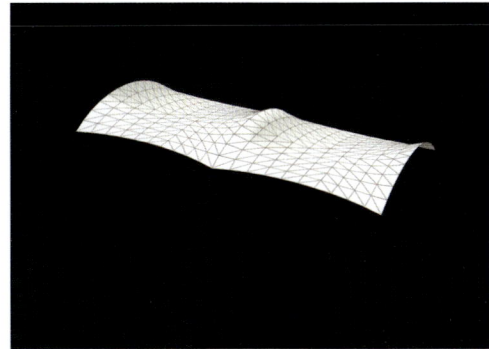
IN-2c. Barrel form.

are usually curved inward 10 to 15 percent of the total length of the span. The cable, belt, or rope is usually inserted in a cable cuff, an edge treatment created either by folding the edge of the material over itself to form a pocket, or by attaching a ready made pocket along the edge. The shallower the curve along the perimeter, the more tension there is in the cable and ultimately in the overall structure and foundation. Very high tension loads require a cable strap treatment, which consists of a continuous clamping of the edge with a series of steel or aluminum straps spaced at specific intervals to support a cable that cannot be inserted in a cable cuff. Cable straps can increase the cost of a fabric structure substantially.

Once the primary points have been determined, the next step is form-finding, or the art and engineering of ascertaining the most efficient structure that can be fabricated with as little waste as possible. In form-finding it is just as important to design a structure that can be easily transported and installed.

There are two methods of form-finding: physical modeling and computer-aided design. Fabric structures may be visualized with physical models or full-scale prototypes, depending on the complexity of the design. Models are created by stretching nylon stockings over wire frames (IN-4). Working with physical models or prototypes enables the designer to view the structure from any angle. However, most fabric structures today are modeled

IN-3. Pier 3 cruise terminal concept, San Juan, Puerto Rico. FTL Design Engineering Studio

IN-4. Physical model study. FTL Design Engineering Studio

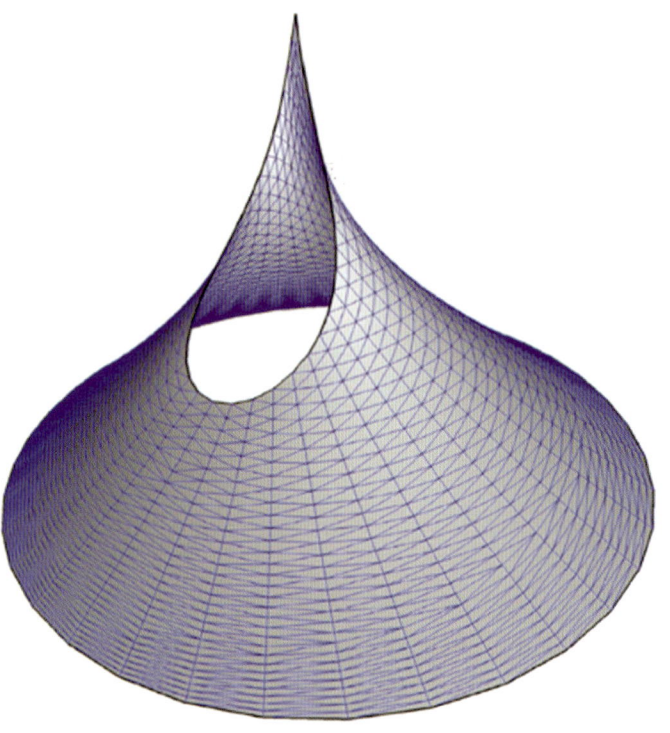

IN-5. Form-finding model. Tensys

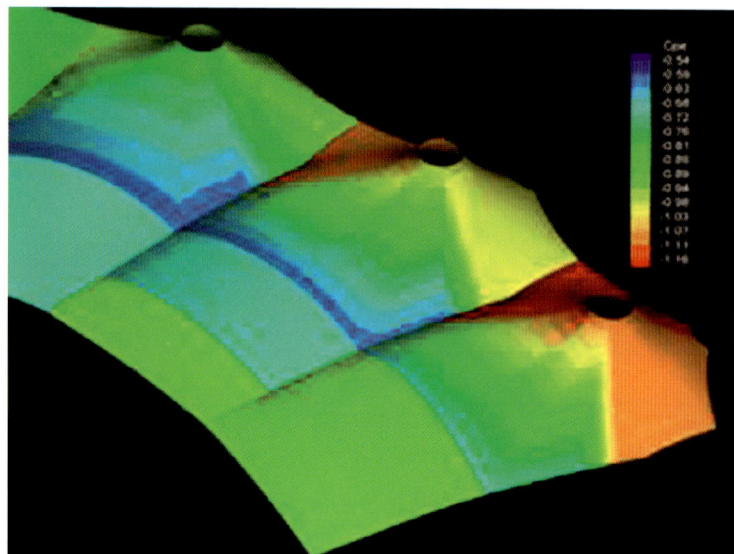

IN-6. Structural analysis model. Tensys

with sophisticated computer software programs (IN-5). These programs allow the designer to create a three-dimensional model that can be viewed at various angles; they also allow customization to provide information for facilitating fabrication and installation. The programs can calculate the amount of fabric required, the dimension of each fabric piece, the size and length of structural members, the size, length, and tension of cables, and the necessary hardware. With a software program the designer can modify the shape more easily than with a physical model.

The last step in the design process is analysis of the structure's response to loads, including dead loads and live loads such as snow, wind, people, and equipment. Structural analysis identifies areas of possible ponding (water collecting on a flat area) and shows where high stresses are located on the structure (IN-6). The analysis enables the designer to determine reactions, size structural members and cables, determine the appropriate fabric, and create computer-generated cutting patterns. Computer patterning is the process of developing a two dimensional representation of a three- dimensional membrane surface. Patterns are created after receiving results of a biaxial test of the specified materials done by the fabricator or provided by the manufacturer to determine the compensation factors required for the specific project. A biaxial test is the testing of a membrane in both the warp (threads running the length of the roll goods) and fill (threads running across the width) direction to calculate the expansion of the material under a given loading condition. Compensation factors are the reduction made to a cutting pattern to allow for the expansion of the membrane once in tension. In some cases, decompensation (addition made to the length of a piece of the membrane which was shortened by compensation) is required in order to meet certain geometric conditions, such as fixed points, where there is no access for tensioning. The panels are sized according to the width of the fabric being used.

MATERIALS

Today's architectural fabrics are composites of woven substrate fiber protected by an applied coating or polymers of films and laminates. New fibers, primarily nylon, polyester, polyethylene and fiberglass, have been developed to meet the need for materials with high strength, long life spans, and a high modulus of elasticity. The woven substrate provides the basic tensile strength of the material and its resistance to tear. The finish coating applied to the substrate material seals the fabric against weather and dirt, provides resistance to UV light, serves as a medium for joining panels, and incorporates fire-resistant properties.

The most important quality in choosing a material for a fabric structure is its fire resistance. National Fire Protection Association (NFPA) 701 is the most common fire test for textiles and films. The American Society for Testing and Materials (ASTM) is another recognized standard for a wide range of materials, and ASTM E-84, 108, and 136 are common tests related to fabrics for membrane structures.

The latest architectural fabrics used for a building envelope respond to heat and light much differently than previous generations of fabric did; they also offer features and benefits different than conventional construction materials (IN-7). Architectural fabrics can be manufactured to vary in translucency from 1 to 95 percent and, in thermal resistance, from that of a single pane of glass to that of a conventionally insulated structure, while still maintaining adequate daylighting. A fabric roof can be a source of interior light at night if artificial light is directed onto its highly reflective surface.

FABRIC SELECTION

The performance of today's architectural fabrics depends upon the weaving pattern, choice of substrate, and coating. Each composite has unique properties and characteristics that suit it to different applications. Most materials presented have a minimum of stretch and shrinkage in a wide range of temperature and humidity conditions, and coatings that prevent mildew, staining, and streaking. Choice of a material calls for understanding of its light reflectivity and light transmission. Reflectivity is the amount of light the surface of the material reflects; transmission is the amount of light that penetrates the material. Most fabrics allow some amount of light transmission, but some materials come with a blackout scrim between layers and allow no light to penetrate, so light and heat from the sun can be controlled.

All the materials come in some shade of white; some are also available in a limited range of colors, depending on supply and demand. The proper selection of membrane material will be based on the proposed size, form, function, and desired longevity of the structure and the economics of the project.

IN-7. Chemical Research Centre, Venafro, Italy. Architect: Samyn and Partners. Canobbio and M. Matteo Piazza

MEMBRANE FABRICATION

The covering of a tensioned fabric structure is referred to as the membrane. It can be fabricated in a number of ways based on the material chosen and the orientation of the seams. All aspects of a fabric structure should be derived from the same computer model or full-scale mockup. Computer-generated patterns are the most widely accepted template for fabrication (IN-8); smaller structures, such as awnings, are patterned directly off a full-scale mockup.

Seams determine the appearance of joined panels. The seams can be sewn, glued, electronically welded, or heat-sealed. Seam styles can be parallel or radial to a mast. *Butt seams* are joints produced by placing two adjacent pieces directly beside one other and covering the joint with a strip of material; *lap seams* are joints made by overlapping the edges of the material. Reinforcements—multiple layers of material applied to specific areas of a membrane to strengthen it where concentrated tension loads exist—are also a part of the fabrication process and differ from project to project.

ARCHITECTURAL FABRICS

Architectural fabrics in common use today include:

- PTFE (polytetrafluorethylene)-coated fiberglass
- Silicone-coated fiberglass
- Woven PTFE
- PVC (polyvinylchloride)-coated polyester
- PVC-laminated polyester
- Theatrical draperies
- Stretch fabrics (spandex)

IN-8. PTFE membrane, Hampton Roads Convention Center, Hampton, Virginia.
FTL Design Engineering Studio

IN-9. Silicone-coated fiberglass membrane, Glasgow Fort Shopping Park, Glasgow, Scotland. PD Interglas

High-density polyethylene (HDPE)

ETFE (ethylenetetrafluorethylene) foil

PTFE-coated fiberglass is the worldwide preferred material for large-scale permanent structures or structures requiring long life and specific construction code compliance (IN-8). PTFE has excellent weather, temperature, and chemical resistance, as well as durability and strength. Its life span is over thirty years, and it is manufactured in accordance with such standards as ASTM E-108 and E-84, meaning that it is noncombustible. PTFE varies in translucence from 7 to 15 percent, and reflects between 68 and 75 percent of incident sunlight. The transmitted light is evenly dispersed and free of shadows and glare.

Before installation, PTFE has an irregular off white or slightly brown color, which is the result of the manufacturing and fabrication process. Once exposed to direct sunlight, its external surface bleaches to a milky white within a matter of days. PTFE comes in colors, but manufacturers require a minimum order. The material requires heat-sealing of FEP (fluorinated ethylene propylene) between layers at the seams to join fabric pattern sections. PTFE is available at 10 to 12 feet wide, depending on the manufacturer. It is considerably more expensive than PVC and is not very flexible. Manufacturers include Saint Gobain, Verseidag, and Fibertech.

Silicone-coated fiberglass is an inexpensive alternative to PTFE fiberglass with many of its attributes. It has very high tensile and tear strength and is more flexible than most other materials. Silicone has had a reputation for years of getting dirty rather quickly and being problematic at the seams; however, the topcoat has been improved and fabricators are willing to use the material. The seaming process requires an adhesive that takes less time to cure completely than PTFE, which reduces labor cost. The seaming process is more efficient and the quality of the seam strength more consistent. Silicone-coated fiberglass does not generate any toxic fumes while burning, which makes it safer than PTFE or PVC. It is long lasting, flame resistant, dimensionally stable, and available in a range of colors and translucence (IN-9). The material comes 6 to 10 feet wide, depending on the manufacturer. Manufacturers include Fabrimax and P-D Interglas.

Woven PTFE is a 100-percent fluoropolymer fabric made with high-strength PTFE. It offers durability, strength, and flexibility. It transmits up to 40 percent of light. It combines good light- and water resistance with the ability to withstand repeated flexing and folding, an advantage over coated fiberglass fabrics. The material is pliable enough for retractable and deployable structures (IN-10). It is rather expensive and is not as strong as

IN-10. Retractable roof, woven PTFE membrane, Castle Kufstein, Kufstein, Austria. Gore

IN-11. PVC membrane, Thomas Moore College Pavilion, Longton, United Kingdom.
Fabric Architecture

IN-12. Awning membrane, Las Vegas Premium Outlet Mall, Las Vegas, Nevada.
Adams Hennon Architects. Fabritec Structures

either PTFE or polyester. This material is available at 6 to 8 feet wide and has a 25-year life span. For colors, a minimum order is required. The manufacturer is W. L. Gore.

PVC-coated polyester is the most cost-effective membrane material and, therefore, an ideal choice for both temporary and permanent tension structures (IN-11). The material is soft, pliable, and less expensive than PTFE. It is available in a variety of weights to meet a wide range of structural requirements. This material is sealed with a radio-frequency (RF) welder or hot air sealer. A number of different topcoats allow panels to be RF welded easily; however, PVC with topcoats of polyvinyl fluoride (PVF) and polyvinylidene fluoride (PVDF), which provide the base material with a much cleaner and maintenance free surface, require additional work in the shop. Both top-of-the-line PVF and PVDF require that the topcoat or film where two panels are to meet be ground off in order for them to be RF welded. This is time consuming and requires great care in order to keep the seams clear of dirt, mold, and mildew. PVC material has a life span range between 15 and 20 years depending on the topcoat chosen. It comes in a variety of colors and translucence. The material can be found as a perforated mesh. PVC is subject to creep—stretching under load—and can also thus require periodic retensioning. The material comes in widths of 54 to 98 inches. Manufacturers include Ferrari, Mehler, Naizil, Seaman, and Verseidag.

PVC-laminated polyester is used primarily for temporary structures and stationary and retractable awnings and canopies. Vinyl laminates are two or more layers of fabric or film joined together by heat, pressure, and a water-based adhesive to form a single ply. These materials are lower in cost and have a shorter life span than coated materials. They come in a variety of colors and in stripes and patterns (IN-12). Fabric is available at 54 to 98 inches wide; the life span is 8 to 10 years. Manufacturers include Herculite and Snyder.

Theatrical draperies are used for interior applications only (IN-13). These are fabrics used primarily in theaters and places of public assembly where fire resistance is required. The materials available vary in quality, texture, width, and cost. Some have very short life spans, while others are manufactured to last a lifetime. Theatrical drapery project do not necessarily need to be in tension. Recommended distributors of theatrical draperies include Rose Brand and Dazian.

Stretch fabrics such as spandex are materials that stretch rather easily in multiple directions. They are used for both temporary and interior projects (IN-14). The material can be dyed or silk screened, and is used often at trade shows and special events. The life span varies depending on the application.

HDPE is manufactured and used in a variety of ways. The material can be made for shading only or engineered and woven for complete water protection. Shade mesh comes in a variety of styles, colors, and shade factors from 50 to 95 percent. A high-density polyethylene fabric provides high tensile strength, ultraviolet (UV) stability, and high UV absorption. Coated polyethylene produces higher strength-to-weight properties than many traditional membrane fabrics. HDPE is 100-percent recyclable since it is a combination of high- and low-density polyethylene. Expected life of the fabric is 10 to 12 years. The shade cloth is available at 8 to 12 feet wide. It is especially well suited to dry and hot climates and where protection from sun and hail is desired (IN-15). Manufacturers include Sunports, Interwrap, and ECP.

ETFE foil is a polymer resin from the same family as PTFE. It is produced in very thin sheets and is manufactured to be installed as inflated pillows, also referred to as cushions or foils. It

IN-14. Gateway atrium membrane. Transformit

IN-13. Shade and bandshell membrane, World Financial Center Winter Garden, New York, New York. FTL Design Engineering Studio

is an alternative to structural glass for long-span structures and, because of its light weight, is a way of reducing the size of the primary structural system (IN-16). ETFE foils are supported by a constant air flow supplied by an inflation system consisting of a centrifugal fan unit and emergency backup, with humidity controls and filters to prevent moisture and dirt from getting inside the pillows. The material has low tear propagation, is UV resistant, and is 100-percent recyclable. Multiple layers of ETFE can provide an effective thermal enclosure. ETFE can be designed with unique patterns on the film, providing a range of light transmission. It can be used in a single layer for smaller structures such as awnings and canopies. Because ETFE requires both fabricating experience and specialized equipment for joining panels, it is best purchased directly through a specialty contractor.

The best way to determine the most appropriate material for your application is by contacting the manufacturers and requesting a fabric sample. Small reference samples of PTFE, PVC, woven PTFE, silicone-coated fiberglass, PVC-coated mesh and HDPE are provided at the back of the book.

COMPONENTS AND DETAILS

One of the beauties of fabric architecture is how few components are required to create a structure: the primary structural support system such as the mast and arch, the fittings and hardware used to tension the membrane, and the membrane itself (IN-17).

IN-16. ETFE membrane, Hanover Stadium, Hanover, Germany. Covertex GmbH

IN-15. Porte cochere, HDPE membrane, Las Vegas Premium Outlet Mall, Las Vegas, Nevada. Fabritec Structures

Most fabric structures require a compression member (mast or arch) to form a complex shape. The member usually has welded cleats or struts that enable it to support the membrane, cable, or other structural components. Masts can terminate on the ground or, in the form of a "flying mast," be supported by a series of cables. Flying masts allow a column-free space in a mast-supported structure.

A base plate forms the connection between the membrane structure and the ground, wall, building, or adjacent structural system (IN-18). The base plate is usually welded to the bottom of a compression member or connected to the mast with a pin connection assembly.

Boss plates, which are steel plates or rings welded to the main plate, are used for localized strengthening of a bolted connection.

Membrane plates are custom-designed plates used to link a membrane to the structural support system. These plates accept membrane catenary cables and pin connection hardware (IN-19). Time-consuming to design, they are the key to a successful tension membrane structure.

A bale ring is a compression ring used to support the membrane on a mast-supported structure. The ring is also used to reduce the stress of the membrane at the top and ease in the fabrication and installation of the membrane (IN-20). Normally, the membrane is clamped to the ring and the entire structure is tensioned at the top by raising the ring. Bale rings vary in shape and size depending on the complexity of the design and the total load to be carried into the support. The ring can be left open for ventilation or covered by a metal, fabric or glass top.

Cables create the edge of tension membrane structures.

IN-17. Detail of shade structure, Dolphin Pool, SeaWorld, Orlando, Florida. Fabritec Structures

IN-18. Base plate detail, Las Vegas Premium Outlet Mall, Las Vegas, Nevada. Fabritec Structures

IN-19. Typical membrane plate. Samuel J. Armijos

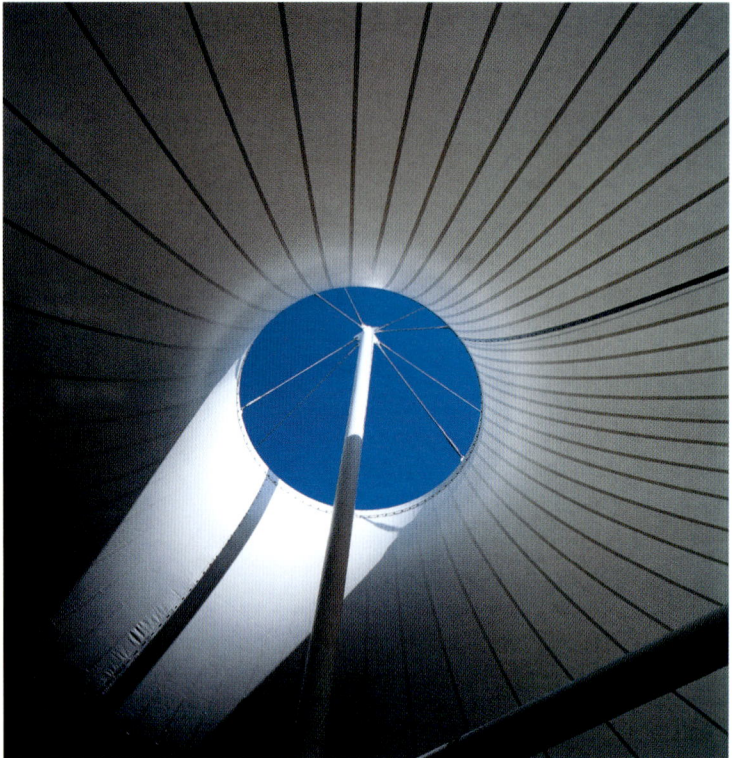

IN-20. Bale ring, Porirua Mall, Wellington, New Zealand. Structurflex

IN-21. Catenary detail, Royal Melbourne Showground, Melbourne, Australia. Structurflex

When located along the perimeter, they are called catenaries; when along the underside of the membrane, they are called the radial or ridge cable; and when over the top of the membrane, valley cables. Catenary cables are the most visible and follow the perimeter stretching from mast to mast (IN-21). They are installed inside a pocket in the membrane or supported along the edge with cable straps. They usually terminate with a threaded rod or forked clevis, a cast pin-connected fitting that is attached to the membrane plates.

Another method of treating the edge of the membrane is with a Keder or roped edge, a unique construction of heavy-duty coated polyester welded to a core of solid PVC, which is attached to the boundaries of the membrane to provide a strong and flexible edge for extrusions and clamping.

Each perimeter mast requires either a large moment connection or a series of cable tiedowns to withstand the loads. Tiedown cables are generally attached to cleats on the top of a mast and connected to anchors installed in the ground with turnbuckles (IN-22).

Fabric structure hardware consists mostly of parts made for the yacht, bridge-building, rigging, and mountain-climbing supply industries. Shackles, turnbuckles, and toggles are just a few of the hardware choices available to link the membrane and the primary structural support (IN-23). Shackles are U-shaped pieces

IN-22. Mast and tiedown detail, 18th and Vine Pavilion, Kansas City, Missouri. Fabritec Structures

(top right) IN-23. Typical hardware assembly. Denver Airport, Denver, Colorado. Samuel J. Armijos

(bottom right) IN-24. Clamping detail, United World College Pool, Singapore. Structurflex

of hardware used in the rigging industry that require a bolted connection with movement in various directions. Turnbuckles and toggles are threaded components used to adjust the length of ropes, wire, rods, and membrane plates.

A fabric clamp is a steel or aluminum profile used to fix the end of a membrane to a curb or join to membranes to each other or to a structural system. Clamp plates of aluminum or steel are normally used to provide a watertight seal along a frame, beam, or adjacent structure. The clamp can be extruded or cast to have a distinct profile (IN-24).

Hardware comes in a variety of finishes and styles. As with the fabrics, the recommended practice is to contact the hardware supplier or manufacturer and request a sample.

INTRODUCTION 23

NOTE ON THE PHOTOGRAPHS

The photographs in *Fabric Architecture* are grouped into the following categories: Awnings and Canopies, Umbrellas, Interior Applications, Tents and Temporary Structures, Shade Structures, Textile Façades, Mast-Supported Structures, Arch- and Frame-Supported Structures, Point-Supported Structures, and Future Structures. The pictures have been provided by the designer, artist, engineer, manufacturer, fabricator, or installer. Information on how to contact them can be found in the Resources section at the end of the book.

For additional information on the fabric structures pictured in this book, write to the credited source of the illustration.

1

AWNINGS AND CANOPIES

An awning is a lightweight, rigid frame clad with fabric that is attached to a building. A canopy is similar to an awning but is self-supporting or attached to the building at a minimal number of locations.

Awnings and canopies have improved markedly with the advent of new materials and framing systems, and today they provide a cost-effective way to transform a building or space. As an architectural element, awnings and canopies come in all shapes and sizes and can be installed relatively easily on both existing structures and new construction. The materials vary in weight, life span, and cost.

Lacing is the traditional technique of attaching a fabric cover to an awning or canopy frame. Grommets are placed along the edge of the membrane, and the cover is tied to the frame by threading rope of an appropriate light weight through the grommets and around a lacing bar, which is attached to the frame. Alternatively, fabric can be attached to the frame by screwing mechanical fasteners directly into the frame with industrial-strength staples that hold the fabric to a specialized frame or extrusion, which is then covered with a custom vinyl strip.

As awnings and canopies become larger, their frames can become complex and visible, which may not be desirable. Designing them with fewer but larger elements that rely on the structural characteristics of the fabric for additional support reduces the amount of visible framework. In the process, a typical awning becomes a tensioned fabric awning.

Main Street awnings, Naples, Florida. Sunmaster of Naples

(opposite) Apple HQ tensioned awnings, United Kingdom. Architen Landrell

City Place Project canopy with Tyler Truss, West Palm Beach, Florida. Eide Industries

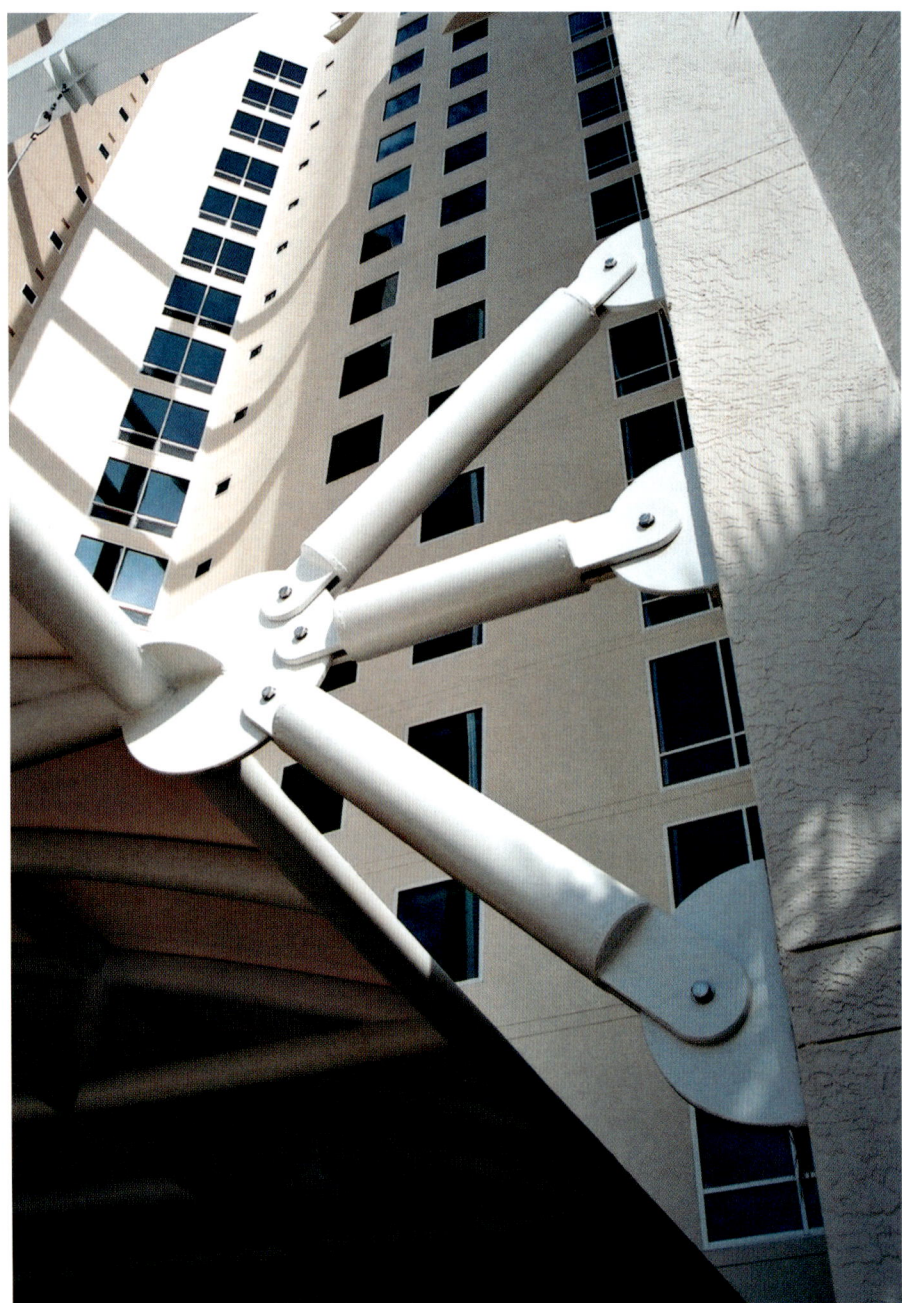

Provence Condominium entry detail, Naples, Florida. Sunmaster of Naples

(top right) Simple shed awning detail, Naples, Florida. Sunmaster of Naples

(bottom right) Arthrex office sail detail, Naples, Florida. Sunmaster of Naples

(opposite) Arthrex office sail detail from below. Sunmaster of Naples

(opposite) **Point Defiance Zoo Kids Zone Wing Canopy.** Rainer Industries

Trilogy Apartment Entry, Philadelphia, Pennsylvania. Fabritec Structures

Provence Condominium entry. Sunmaster of Naples

AWNINGS AND CANOPIES 33

Ballston Retail entry, Arlington, Virginia.

Fabritec Structures

Fullers Ferry Terminal, Auckland, New Zealand.

Structurflex

Florida Atlantic University building entry, Boca Raton, Florida. Fabritec Structures

Entrance to DuSable Hall at Northern Illinois University, DeKalb, Illinois. Fabritec Structures

AWNINGS AND CANOPIES 35

St. Charles Youth Park, St. Charles, Illinois.
Lawrence Fabric Structures

Orlando International Airport toll booth canopy, Orlando, Florida. Fabritec Structures

Horsecreek Carport, Naples, Florida.
Sunmaster of Naples

Multiple striped awnings on an office building, Naples, Florida. Sunmaster of Naples

Le Rivage condominium porte cochere, Naples, Florida. Sunmaster of Naples

Striped canopy. Ferrari Textiles

Building canopy, Arbee Associates, Gaithersburg, Maryland. FTL Design Engineering Studio

12th Street Marketplace Atrium, Los Angeles, California.
Fabritec Structures

Awnings, Caesars Palace, Las Vegas, Nevada.
Fabritec Structures

Awning, Martin House, Naples, Florida.
Sunmaster of Naples

AWNINGS AND CANOPIES 39

Pool canopy, Le Rivage condominium, Naples, Florida.
Sunmaster of Naples

Interior of rooftop bar and Bistro Vindeset, St. Louis, Missouri.
Lawrence Fabric Structures

Esplanade awning, Naples, Florida. Sunmaster of Naples

Entry, Caribe and Cove Towers, Naples, Florida.
Sunmaster of Naples

Port Royal Club, Naples, Florida. Sunmaster of Naples

42 FABRIC ARCHITECTURE

Four-Corners Retail Mall, West Los Angeles, California. Eide Industries

Cobre Valley High canopy. Fabritec Structures

(above left) **Walkway, Edgewater Ferry Terminal, Edgewater, New Jersey.** Fabritec Structures

(above right) **Detail of blue awning, Palazzo resort, Los Angeles, California.** Eide Industries

Butterfly entry, Children's Hospital, St. Louis, Missouri.
Lawrence Fabric Structures.

Ground view of Founders' Center Canopy, Straubing, Germany. Cenotec

Balcony view of Founders' Center Canopy, Straubing, Germany. Cenotec

AWNINGS AND CANOPIES 45

Canopy, Coastal Grand Mall, Myrtle Beach, South Carolina. Eide Industries

Glasgow Fort Shopping Park, panoramic view, Glasgow, Scotland. PD Interglas

The Lights–Cricklade College Theater, Andover, Hampshire, United Kingdom. J. J. Carter

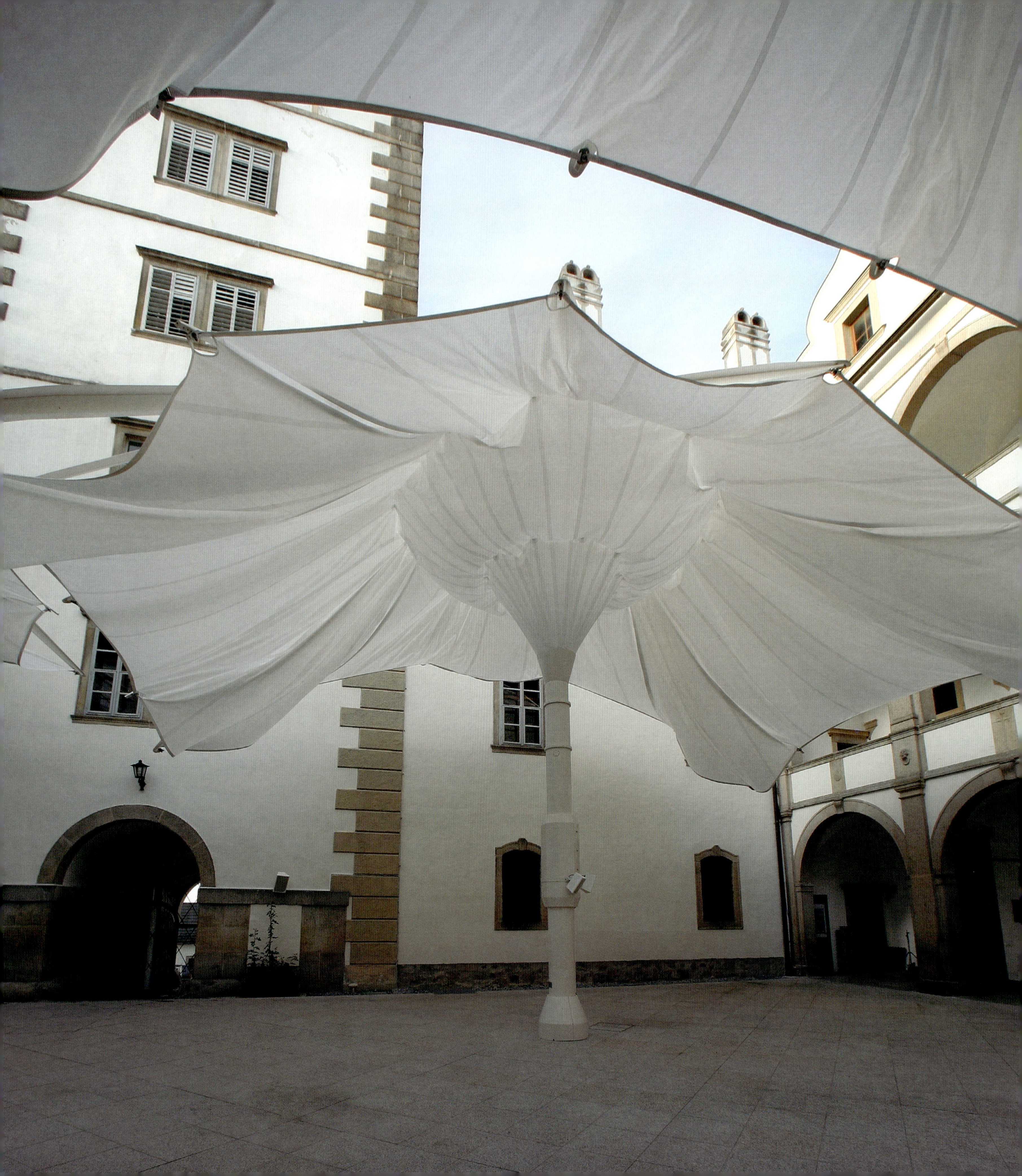

2

UMBRELLAS

An umbrella is a canopy supported by a single mast designed to protect users from sun and precipitation. Umbrellas are engineered for a variety of environments and purposes. The support structures are usually steel, aluminum, or wood, can be almost any size, and may be fixed or collapsible. The perimeter or edge of the fabric may be scalloped or rigid, the top open or closed. Foundations are required to support most umbrellas; however, a ground sleeve, which is a pipe slightly larger than the umbrella column, can also be used.

Umbrellas normally have either four, six, or eight sides supported by a series of cantilever arms of equal length that come off the center mast, or they may consist of a circular frame supported by a series of cables or rods, much like a bicycle wheel. Umbrellas may be installed in groups, separately, or close enough to be attached to each other. They may comprise multiple units with repetitive frame elements that support one large cover, or the mast may be located on one side, supporting the umbrella from above, to provide a column-free space (see top left image, page 65).

An inverted umbrella has a membrane that slopes toward its center support rather than the perimeter. Inverted umbrellas normally are designed to allow water to drain into the center support, to be discharged elsewhere.

Today's computer patterning programs easily create membrane tops for unique umbrellas with cantilever arms of varying lengths, heights, and slopes.

Type E inverted umbrella. MDT-TEX

Pow Wow umbrellas, Mystic Lake Casino, Prior Lake, Minnesota. Fabritec Structures

(top left) **Auto dealership umbrellas by day, Essex, United Kingdom.** Fabric Architecture

(top right) **Auto dealership umbrellas at night.** Fabric Architecture

Auto dealership umbrellas in pairs. Fabric Architecture

Dallas Executive Airport, Dallas, Texas. Fabritec Structures

Fabric structures, Louisville Park, Louisville, Kentucky. Fabritec Structures

Umbrellas of varying heights and colors. Sunports

Highway tollbooth membrane structure, Tiantai, China. Fabrimax

UMBRELLAS 53

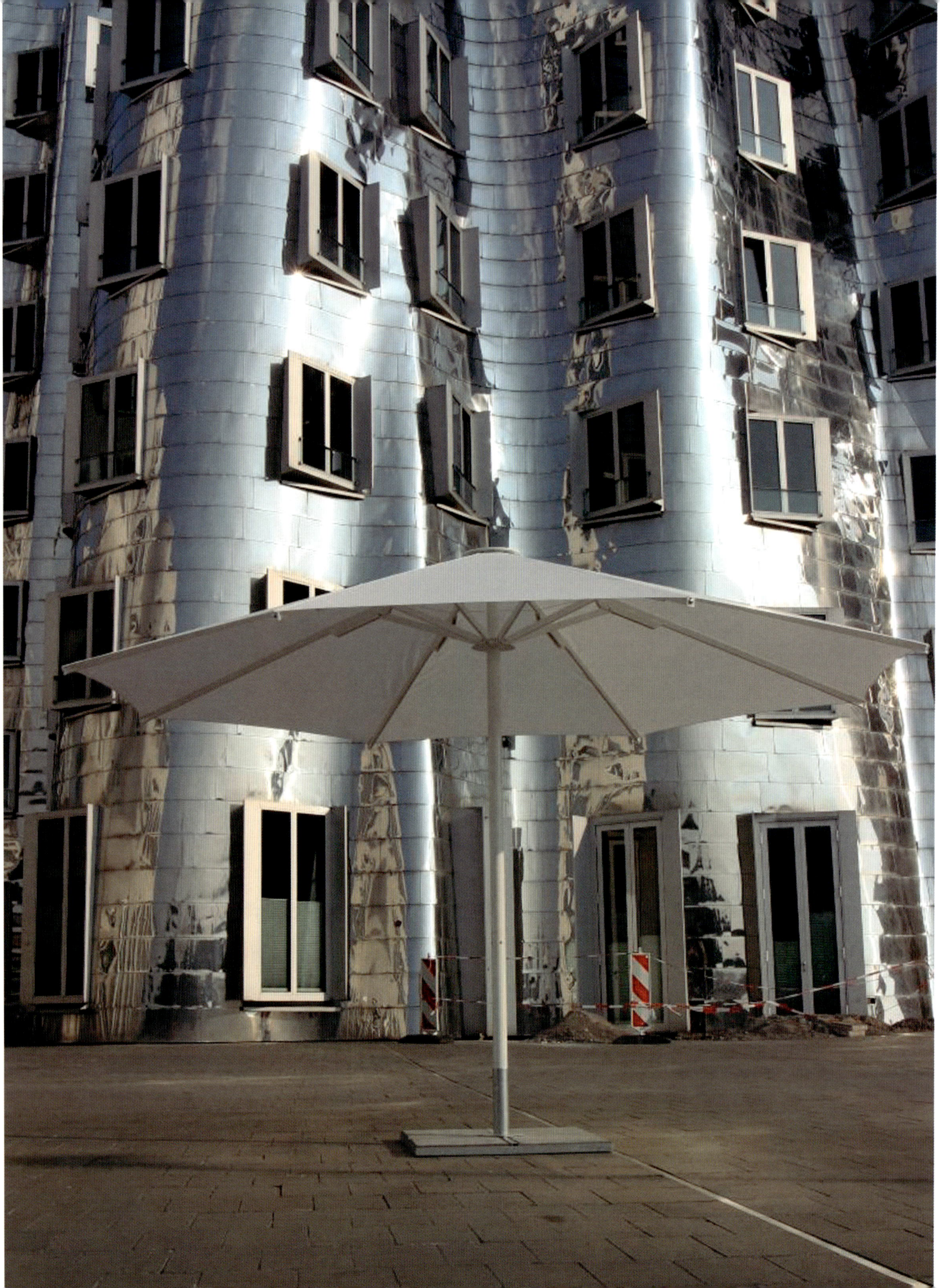

(opposite) **Type T umbrella.** MDT-TEX

Hypar umbrella. Sunports

Sandown Park Racecourse, view from below, Surrey, United Kingdom. J. J. Carter

Sandown Park Racecourse, perspective view. J. J. Carter

(top left) **Bahama Beach Coolbrellas, Dallas, Texas.** Sunports

(top right) **Landscape umbrellas, Sara Lee headquarters, Winston-Salem, North Carolina.** Fabritec Structures

Custom inverted umbrellas, Staten Island, New York.
FTL Design Engineering Studio

Inverted umbrellas with graphics. MDT-TEX

Restaurant umbrellas joined together. Ferrari Textiles

UMBRELLAS 57

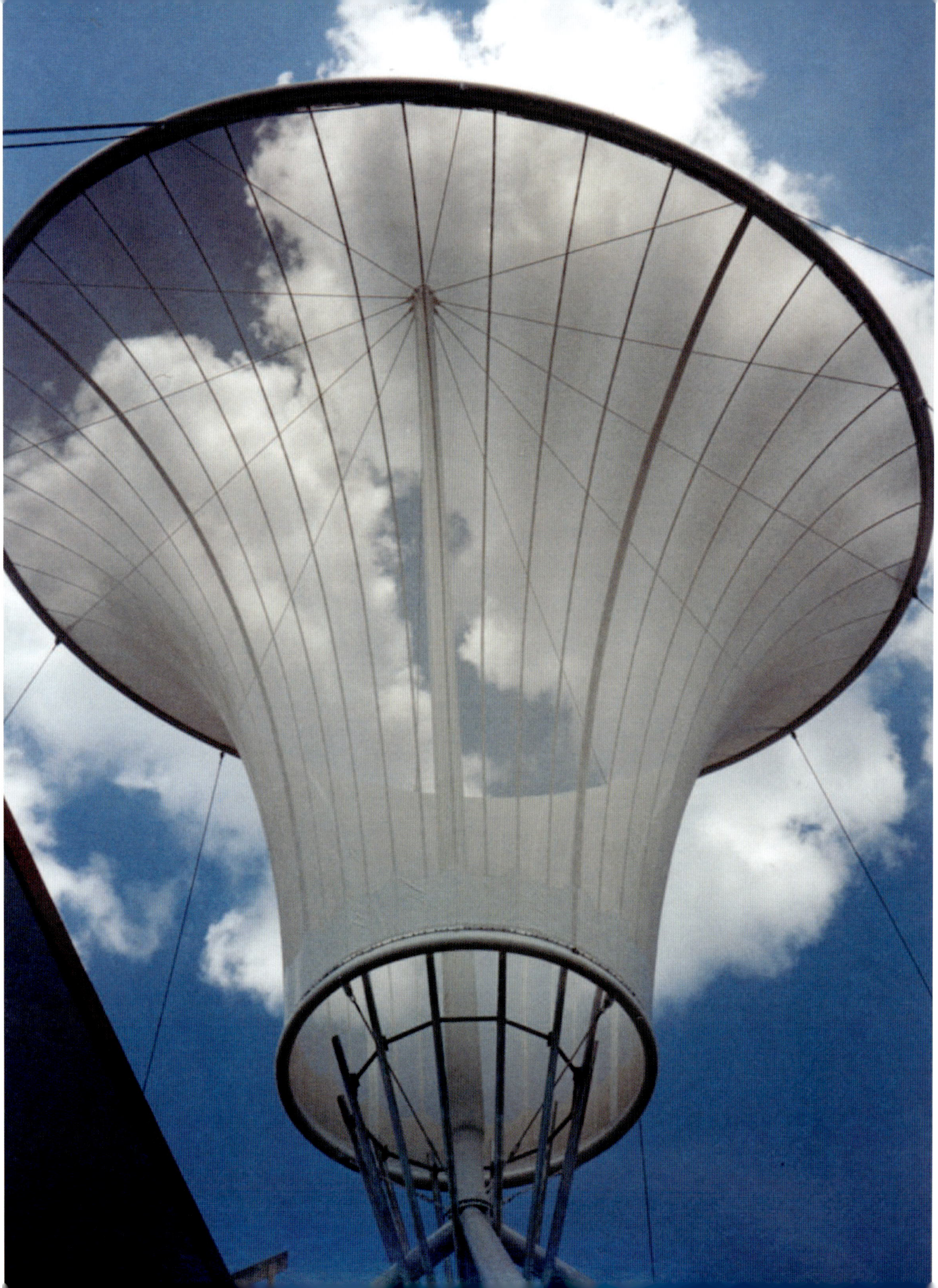

(opposite) **Carnegie Science Center by day, Pittsburgh, Pennsylvania.** FTL Design Engineering Studio

Chamber of Commerce umbrellas by day, Wurzburg, Germany. Covertex GmbH

(below left) **Detail of Chamber of Commerce umbrellas.** Covertex GmbH

(below right) **Chamber of Commerce umbrellas at night.** Covertex GmbH

UMBRELLAS 59

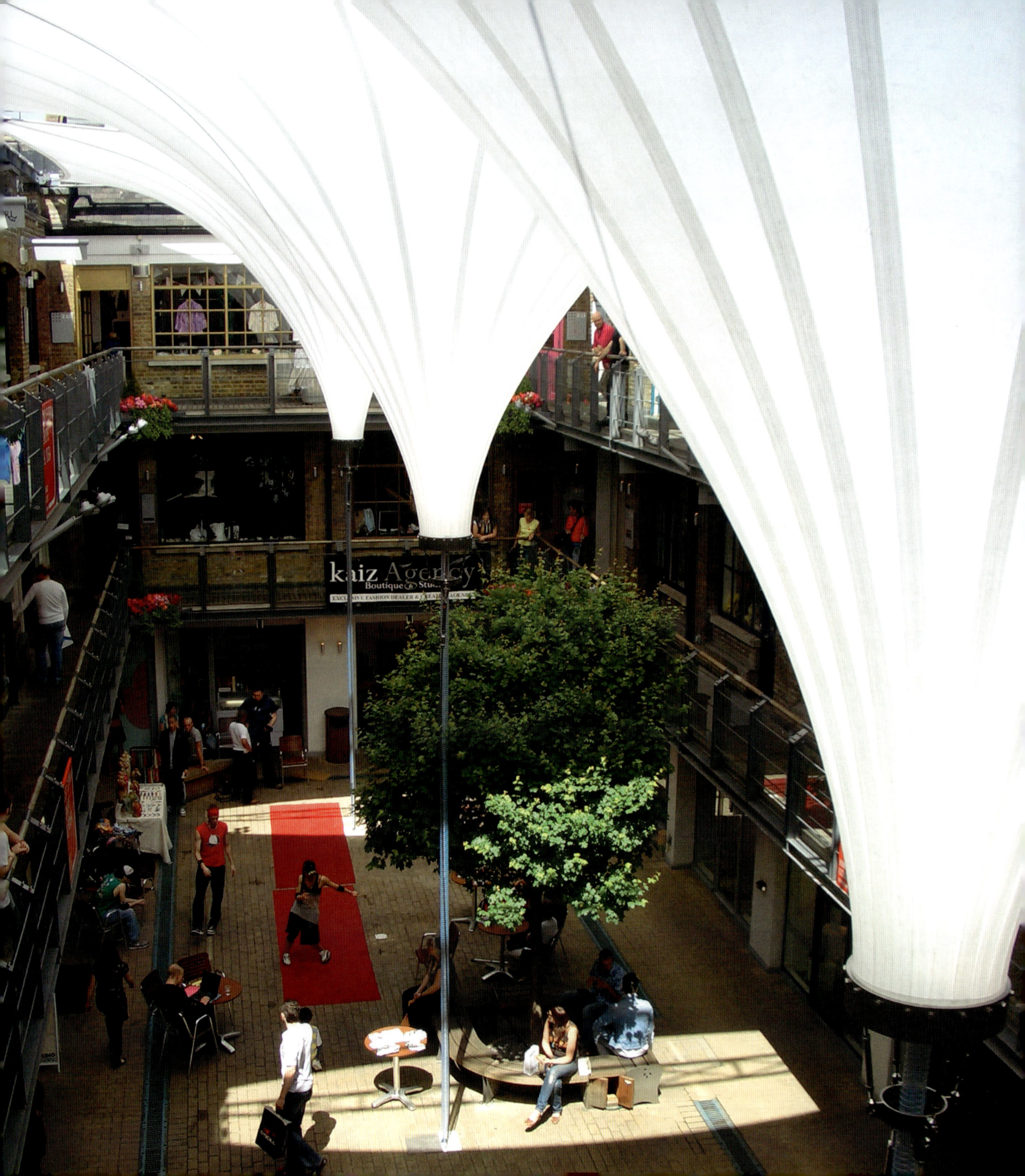
kaiz Agency
Boutique & Studio

Butterfly umbrellas. MDT-TEX

(opposite) Fabric structures, Kingly Court, London, United Kingdom.
Architen Landrell

Multi-umbrella structure, rear view, Cogi Farms, Pawling, New York. Fabritec Structures

Multi-umbrella structure, Cogi Farms. Fabritec Structures

UMBRELLAS 61

Retractable umbrellas closed, Weitra Castle, Weitra, Austria. Gore

(opposite) Retractable umbrellas open, Weitra Castle. Gore

(below left) Retractable umbrellas almost closed, Weitra Castle. Gore

(below right) Retractable umbrellas almost open, Weitra Castle. Gore

62   FABRIC ARCHITECTURE

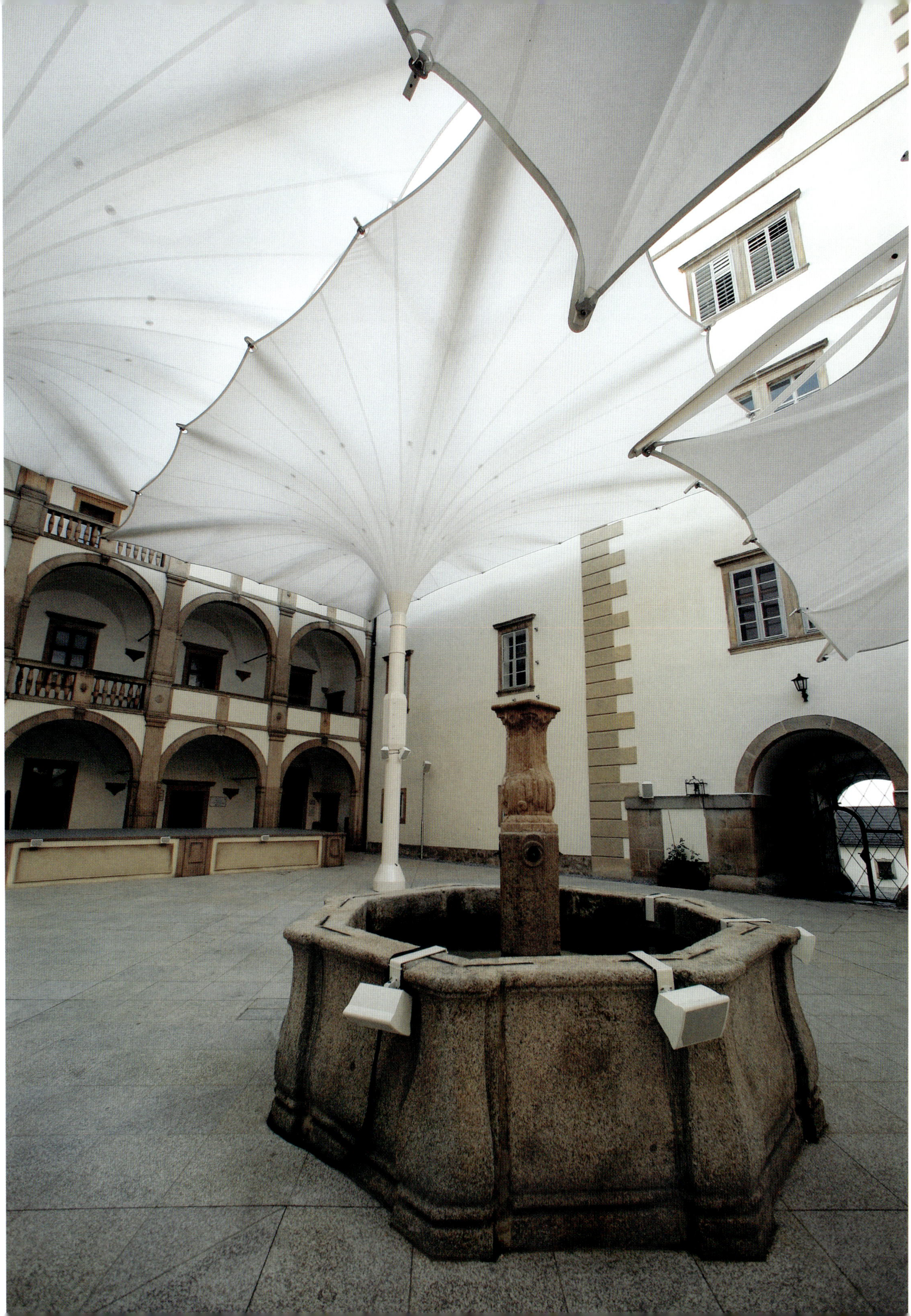

Retractable umbrellas in blue, Weitra Castle.
Gore

Retractable umbrellas in orange, Weitra Castle.
Gore

Retractable umbrellas in purple, Weitra Castle.
Gore

Detail of retractable umbrellas, Weitra Castle. Gore

64   FABRIC ARCHITECTURE

Sidearm umbrella. MDT-TEX

Flemington Auto dealership umbrella, Flemington, New Jersey. Fabritec Structures

Inverted umbrellas, Potsdam, Germany. Fibertech

UMBRELLAS 65

Expo98 umbrellas, front view. Designer: Salgado. Canobbio and M. Matteo Piazza

Umbrella Bar at ski resort. MDT-TEX

Stratford Bus Interchange at night, Stratford, London, United Kingdom. Architen Landrell

66 FABRIC ARCHITECTURE

Detail of foldable umbrellas at private residence, Dubai. Cenotec

Foldable umbrellas at private residence, Dubai. Cenotec

UMBRELLAS 67

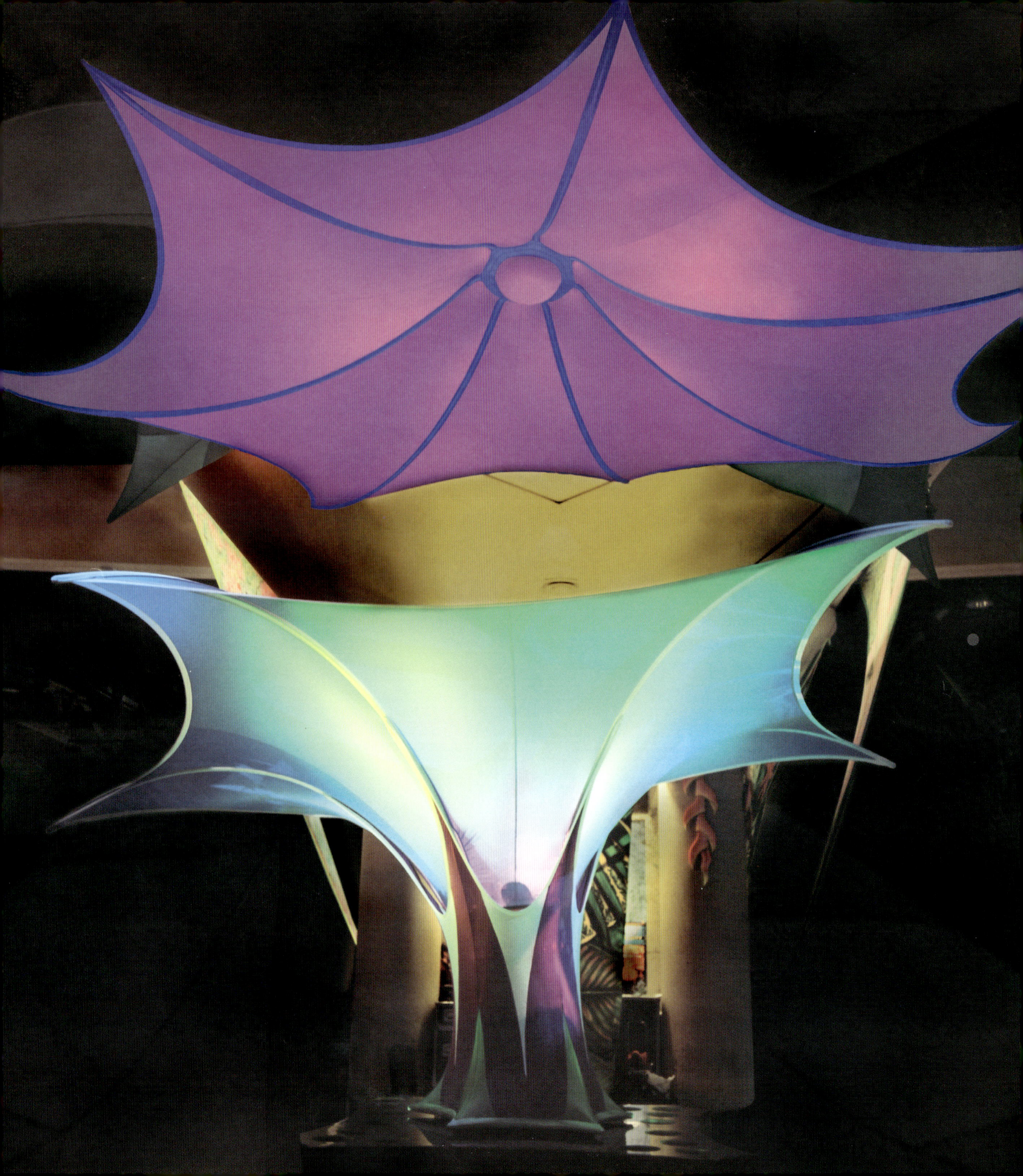

3

INTERIOR APPLICATIONS

Interior fabric structures comprise walls, ceilings, and three-dimensional sculptures, used alone or in combinations. They can be temporary or permanent. Some have acoustical properties; most are intended as sculptural forms, or for lighting or signage. They are designed primarily for aesthetic purposes, but they must be compatible with such equipment as sprinklers and electrical and mechanical systems and must meet the requirements of building, lighting, and fire codes. When used in an existing building, they must be attached to or supported by structural elements that can absorb their specific loads.

Fabric used for interior applications usually is limited to materials that "breathe," because ventilation is a major concern indoors. Because lighting and mechanical systems are often required above and below the structures, they must be designed and installed so as not to prohibit air movement or present other safety issues.

Interior fabric structures also are usually constructed from elastic fabrics that can be stretched easily into shapes with double curvature, though not all need to have double curvature: they may be constructed much like a billboard, office partition, or room divider. Fabric walls can hang from the ceiling like curtains or be tensioned from the floor and ceiling with adjustable turnbuckles. They can be self-supporting or hang from a structural beam.

Finally, interior fabric structures may have graphics applied to them or be digitally printed. Lighting may be from above, below, in front, behind, or even from within the structure itself (see, for example, bottom image, page 70).

Star Twisters, Top of the Hub Restaurant, Boston, Massachusetts. Transformit

Dynamics wall and ceiling system. Transformit

Dynamics at trade show, view from above. Transformit

Detail of Dynamics wall system. Transformit

INTERIOR APPLICATIONS 71

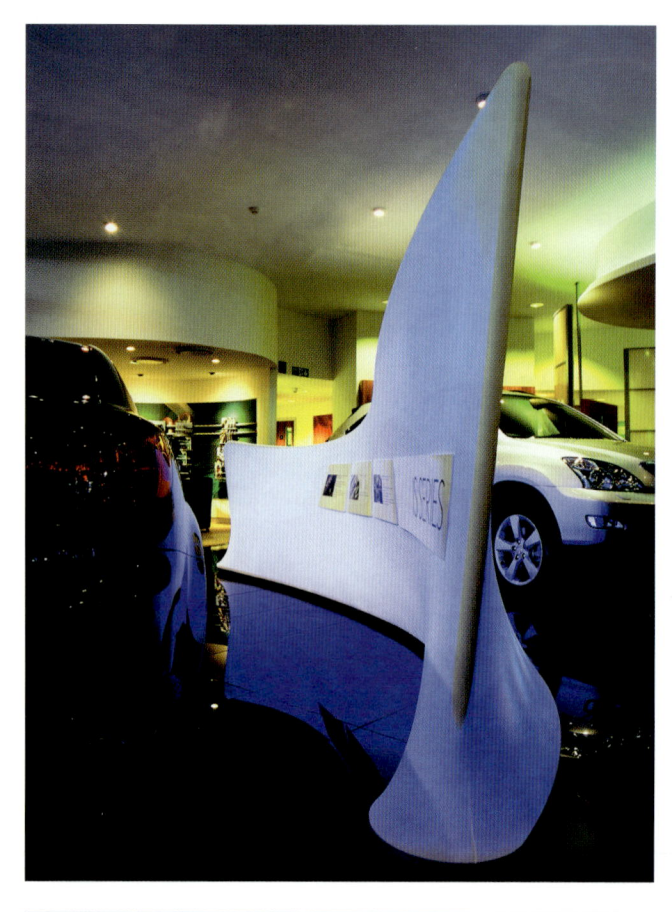

(above left) **Lexus IS Series Launch fabric wall system, throughout the United Kingdom.** Architen Landrell

(above right) **Hanging Zurich lamps.** Gisela Stromeyer Architectural Design

Screened wall system, Paul Mitchell event. Pink Inc.

Star Drops, Sony Plaza, New York, New York. Transformit

Star Drops at IBM event. Transformit

Fabric sails at Kingswalk Shopping Centre, Gloucester, United Kingdom. Architen Landrell

INTERIOR APPLICATIONS   73

Specialty free-form wing system.
Transformit

Tree of Life fabric sculpture. Pink Inc.

74 FABRIC ARCHITECTURE

Liner at O2 Entry Plaza, London, United Kingdom. Architen Landrell

Fabric ceiling with recessed light fixtures. Ferrari Textiles

(below left) **Meeting room with fabric ceiling, Mairie d'Antony, France.** Ferrari Textiles

(below right) **Curved ceiling panels, Reuters Building, Canary Wharf, London, United Kingdom.** Architen Landrell

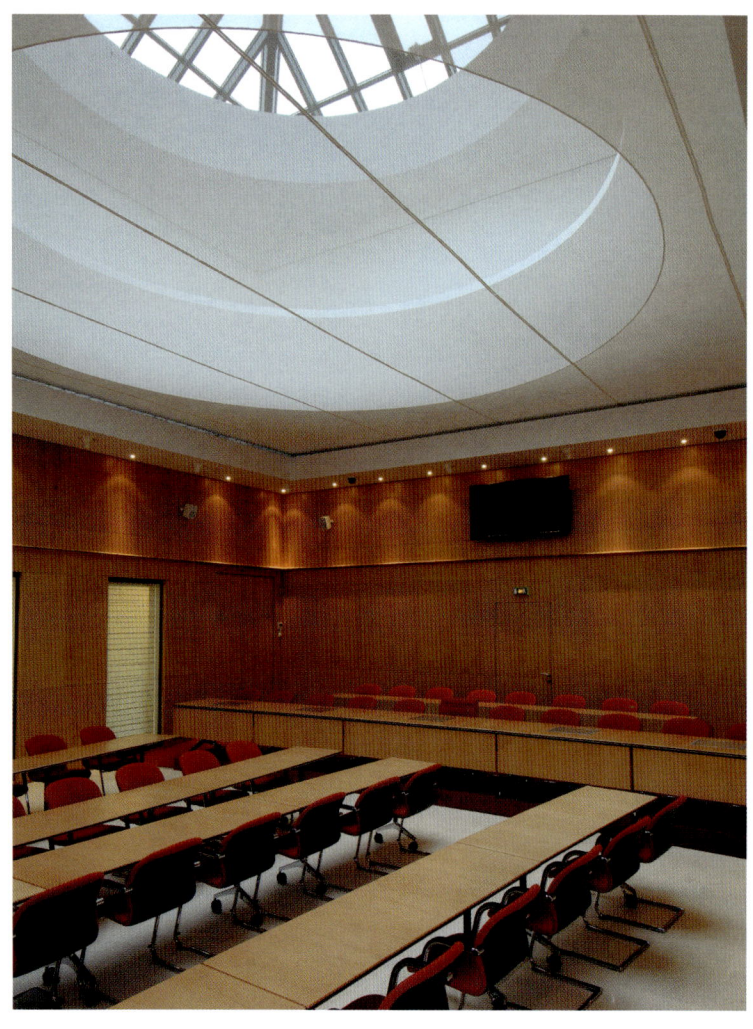

Fabric panels, Halles de Wazemmes, Lille, France. Ferrari Textiles

Restaurant canopy, British Museum, London, United Kingdom. Architen Landrell

Ceiling hypars in office, London, United Kingdom. Architen Landrell

INTERIOR APPLICATIONS

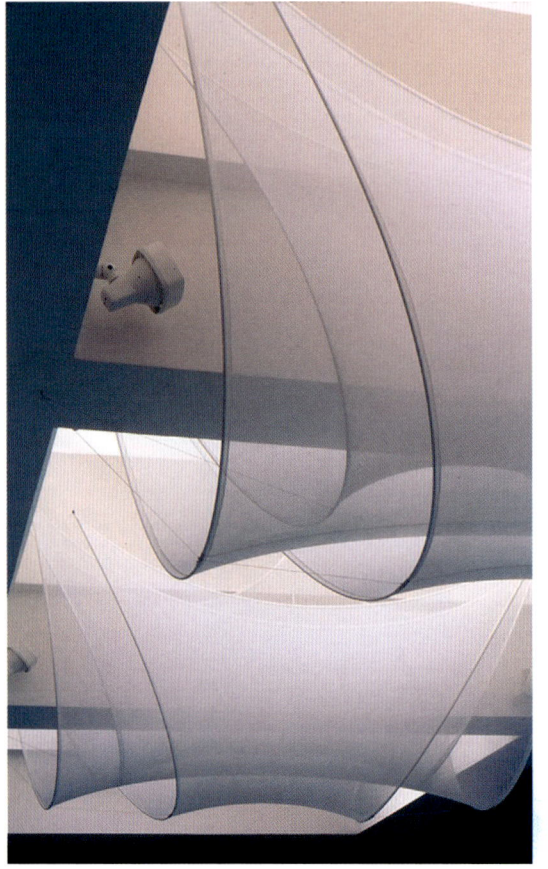

Fabric ceiling, Equinox Pool, New York, New York. Gisela Stromeyer Architectural Design

(bottom left) Detail of fabric ceiling in office interior, New York, New York. Gisela Stromeyer Architectural Design

(bottom right) **Circle Surround wall system.** Pink Inc.

78   FABRIC ARCHITECTURE

(above left) **Fabric structures, perspective view, Organics. Orange County Convention Center, Orlando, Florida.**
Transformit

(above right) **Fabric structures, view from below, Organics.**
Transformit

GES hanging cubes. Fabric Images

INTERIOR APPLICATIONS 79

Lanterns, Great Indoors store, throughout USA. Transformit

Corridor, Collaborate office, San Francisco, California. Design: Huntsman AG. David Wakely Photographer. Gisela Stromeyer Architectural Design

Fabric tower, Banque Populaire de L'Atlantique, France. Ferrari Textiles

80 FABRIC ARCHITECTURE

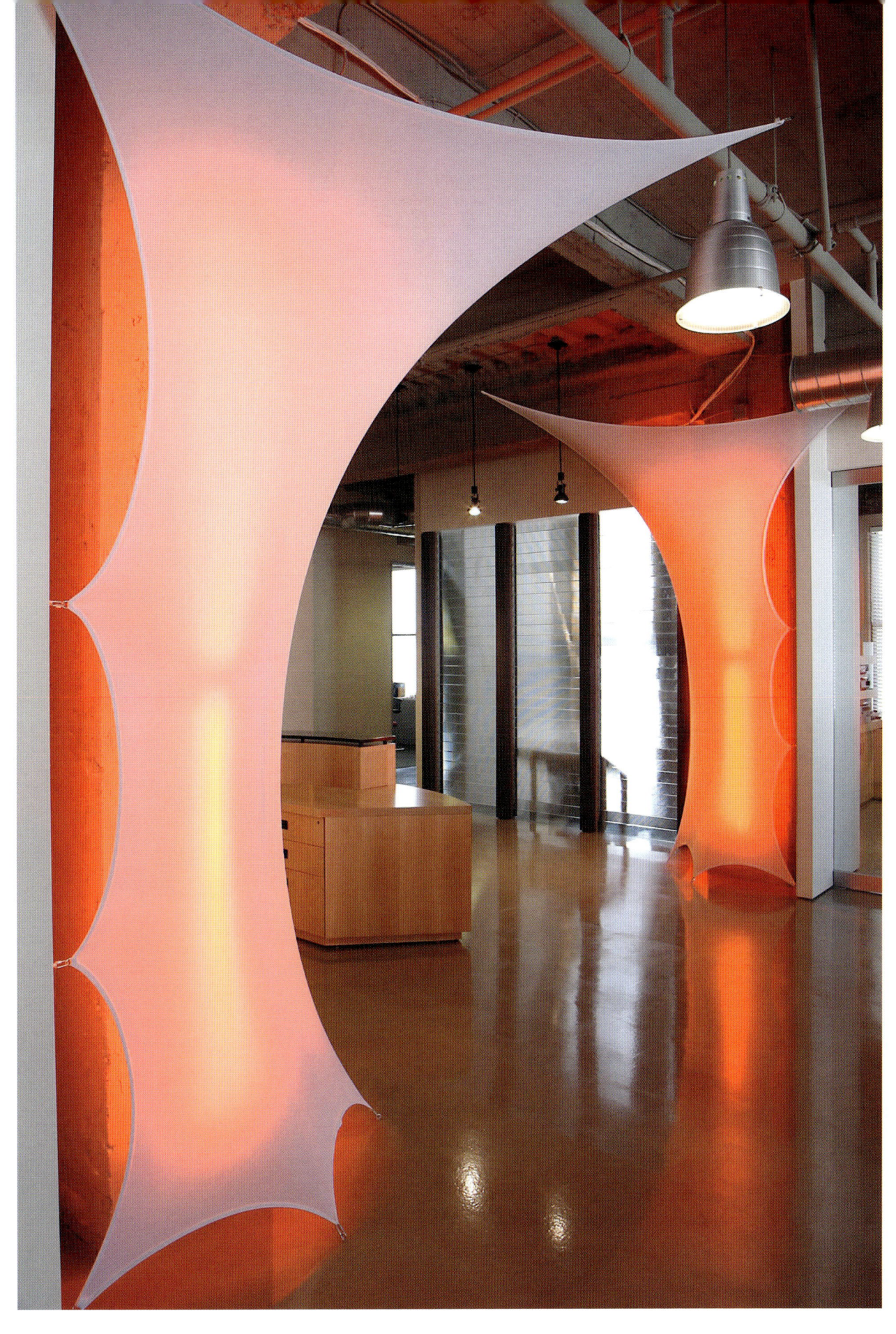

Column detail, Collaborate office. Design: Huntsman AG. David Wakely Photographer. Gisela Stromeyer Architectural Design

INTERIOR APPLICATIONS 81

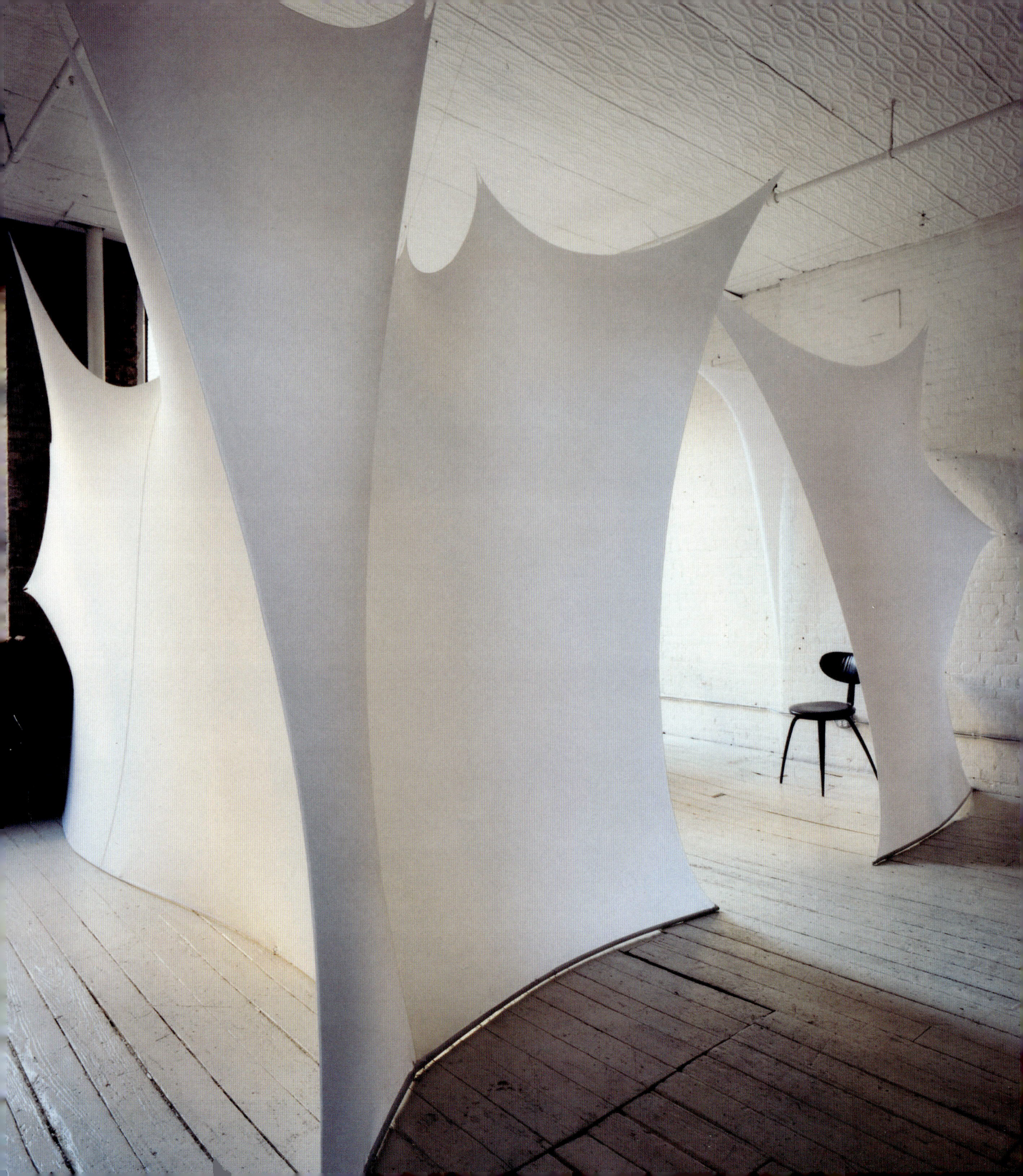

Fashion event at Elie Tahari, New York, New York Gisela Stromeyer Architectural Design

(opposite) Threefold wall in office, New York, New York. Gisela Stromeyer Architectural Design

Loft interior, Roth residence, New York, New York. Gisela Stromeyer Architectural Design

INTERIOR APPLICATIONS

Mixitup showroom.
Fabric Images

Fabric ribbon at Imperial War Museum, Duxford, United Kingdom. Architen Landrell

84   FABRIC ARCHITECTURE

BBC Bandshell interior, London, United Kingdom. Architen Landrell

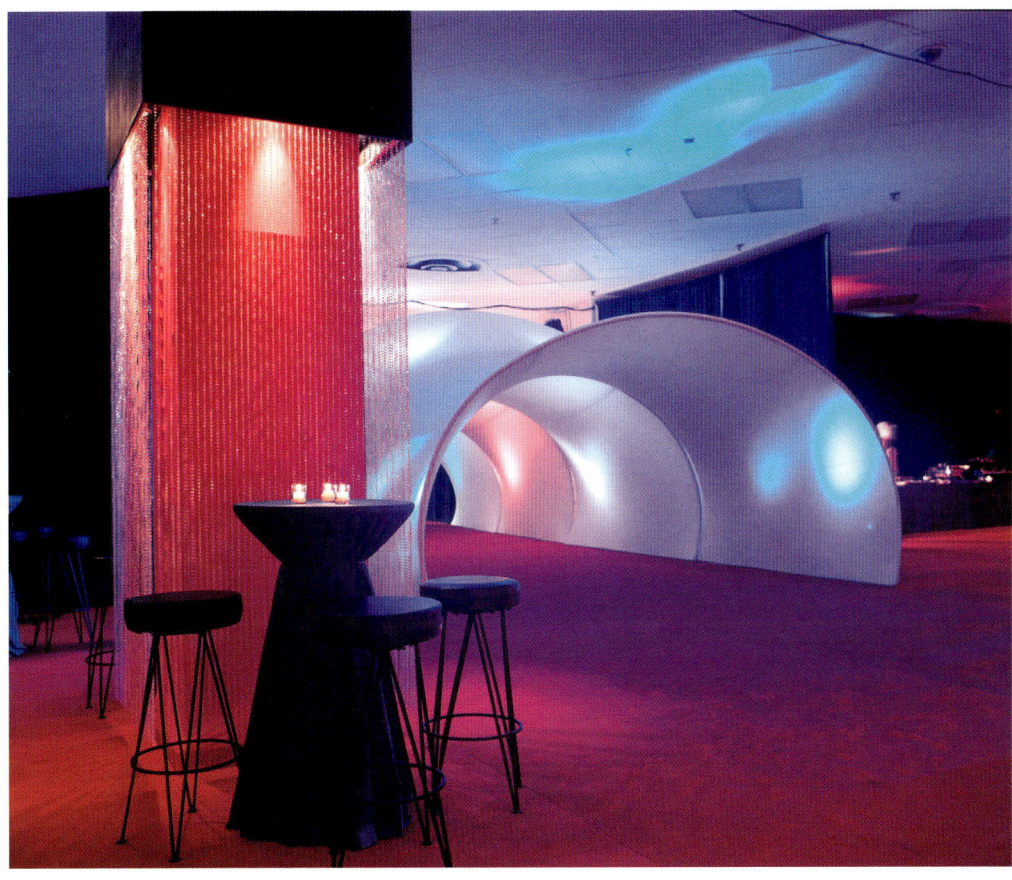

Wave Tunnel system, backlit. Pink Inc.

INTERIOR APPLICATIONS 85

(above left) **Office interior with graphics on wall.** Fabric Images

(above right) **Photos on floating disks.** Fabric Images

Incognito Club, Zurich, Switzerland. Gisela Stromeyer Architectural Design

Custom fabric structures for Grammy Awards party.

Gisela Stromeyer Architectural Design

Grammy Awards party structure, backlit.

Gisela Stromeyer Architectural Design

INTERIOR APPLICATIONS 87

Interior of exhibitor's booth. Fabric Images

Wall detail of exhibitor's booth. Fabric Images

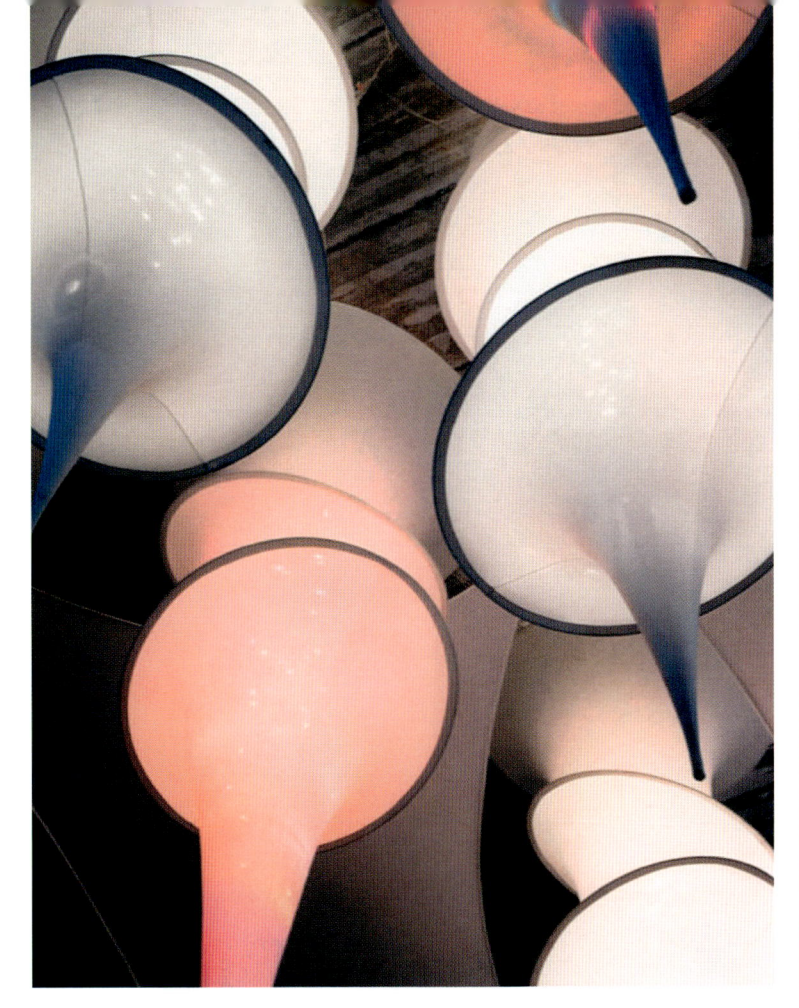

(above left) **Detail of hanging Zurich lamps.** Gisela Stromeyer Architectural Design

(above right) **Hanging custom fabric rosettes.** Fabric Images

Hanging columns, MG Design. Fabric Images

INTERIOR APPLICATIONS 89

Column fabric floor lamps.
Gisela Stromeyer Architectural Design

Morning Glory fabric structures. Transformit

90 FABRIC ARCHITECTURE

(above left) **Trade show booth with sheer fabric.** Transformit

(above right) **Fi-Fi Awards stage set and ceiling, Hammerstein Ballroom, New York, New York.** Pink Inc.

Fabric ceiling panels, Denunzio Pool, Princeton University, Princeton, New Jersey. Architects: Hillier. Fabritec Structures

INTERIOR APPLICATIONS 91

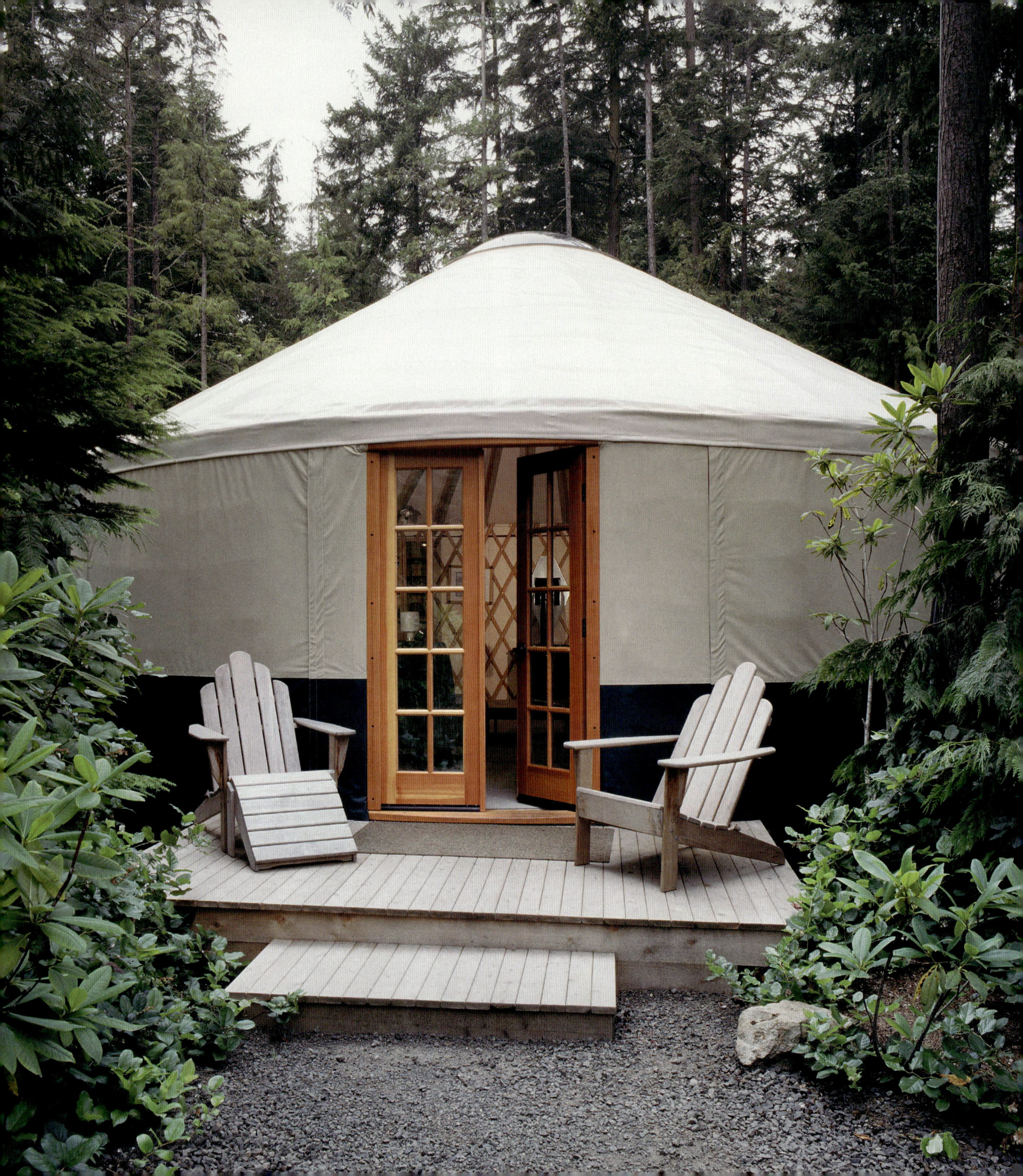

4

TENTS AND TEMPORARY STRUCTURES

Tents are the oldest and most versatile form of shelter and come in all types, shapes, and sizes, from one-person camping tents to clear spans that can house many thousands. Tents are usually categorized as frame tents, pole tents, or tension tents. A frame tent is an assembled framework made of aluminum or steel pipes that support the fabric roof. A pole tent features a set of individual poles arranged beneath the fabric roof to support and define the shape of the structure. A tension tent shares some characteristics with the pole tent, but relies more on the tensioning of the fabric roof for its structural integrity and shape. Tents normally have interior columns. The larger the tent, the more it relies on the fabric's structural properties.

When a tent includes mechanical, lighting, and flooring systems, it becomes a temporary structure. Temporary structures have temporary foundations. Frame and pole tents normally are anchored in the ground by means of rope or webbing belts held by stakes and sand bags. Tension tents and clear spans that must support greater loads use high-strength belts or wire rope for tensioning and are anchored with stakes, augers, or weights made of concrete, steel, or even water.

Clear-span structures, which have no interior columns, use steel or aluminum modular trusses or beams, generally with simple connecting members for ease of assembly (see center image, page 105). The covering is made of a series of fabric panels that are tensioned through extruded channels in the frame. These structures can be designed for snow load by using heavier fabric, larger beam sections, and additional support hardware. A foundation is not required to anchor a clear span, but a small footing pad is recommended.

Skyscape, Millennium Dome, London, United Kingdom. Architen Landrell

Tensioned tent structure at dusk. HDO

Cavalia Tent at night, Travels Throughout the World. FTL Design Engineering Studio

Tent resembling a steamboat. HDO

TENTS AND TEMPORARY STRUCTURES   95

Interior fabric ceiling at Bryant Park Fashion Show, New York, New York. FTL Design and Engineering Studio

Tent with specialized lighting. Main Attractions

96 FABRIC ARCHITECTURE

Clear vinyl ceiling interior of frame tent system. Anchor Industries

Tent with interior liner. Main Attractions

TENTS AND TEMPORARY STRUCTURES 97

Clear span system for Galerie Mayer event. Anchor Industries

Clear vinyl ceiling interior of a clear span. Anchor Industries

Navitrac tent system. Anchor Industries

98   FABRIC ARCHITECTURE

Polygon Series clear span with high, translucent fabric ceiling panels. Universal Fabric Structures

Clear span structure on pier. Tentnology

Band performing under a flying mast tent. Tentnology

100   FABRIC ARCHITECTURE

20-foot-square Marquee flying mast tent with water ballast. Tentnology

Multiple Century frame tents. Anchor Industries

Frame tent used for wedding reception. Main Attractions

Multiple tents for a Formula 1 event, Bahrain.
Tentnology

Outdoor classroom, Elmlea School, Bristol, United Kingdom. Architen Landrell

Pre-engineered clear span system with rounded end. Universal Fabric Structures

Aerial view of clear span used for movie premiere overlooking New York City. Main Attractions

Pre-engineered clear span used as ferry terminal. Main Attractions

TENTS AND TEMPORARY STRUCTURES 103

Clear span tent with hard side walls at dusk. Main Attraction

Pre-engineered clear span in desert, closeup view. Main Attraction

Pre-engineered clear span in desert, distant view. Main Attraction

104   FABRIC ARCHITECTURE

Temporary tent, Bryant Park Ice Rink, New York, New York.

Samuel J. Armijos

Interior of pre-engineered clear span showing lighting, clear and solid fabric and fabric-clad tables. Anchor Industries

Anchor/Roder structure with cathedral side walls. Anchor Industries

TENTS AND TEMPORARY STRUCTURES 105

(above left) **Velux Lounge on the Medienbunker, Hamburg, Germany.** Cenotec

(above right) **Interior of Anchorspan structure showing little or no interior framing.** Anchor Industries

Anchorspan structure with vestibule. Anchor Industries

Anchorspan on grass with no side walls. Anchor Industries

20-foot-square traditional striped frame tent. Anchor Industries

A series of 15-foot-square traditional frame tents by a pool. Anchor Industries

Clear span with shading material at Loma Linda University, Loma Linda, California. Fabritec Structures

TENTS AND TEMPORARY STRUCTURES 107

Temporary stage cover, Monschau Castle, Monschau, Germany. Cenotec

Front view of arch tent, Guarda, Portugal. Cenotec

108 FABRIC ARCHITECTURE

A tent with multiple frames and tops. This structure is set up as a frame tent. Anchor Industries

A tent with multiple frames and tops set up as a tension tent. Anchor Industries

Tensioned rental tent at night. Main Attractions

60-foot-wide tension tent. Anchor Industries

TENTS AND TEMPORARY STRUCTURES 109

(above left) **Single teepee.** Anchor Industries

(above right) **Classic camp tent with fly.** Anchor Industries

Classic yurt. Rainier Industries

110 FABRIC ARCHITECTURE

Pole tent at horse farm. Anchor Industries

Tent in Zanzibar. Naizil

Party tent with clear top. Anchor Industries

Interior of a tension tent with covered columns, ceiling liner, and custom mural. HDO

112 FABRIC ARCHITECTURE

Polynesian-style cabana. Eide Industries

Tuscan-style cabana. Eide Industries

Temporary structure, Buckingham Palace, London, United Kingdom. Hopkins Architects. Architen Landrell

Central Park summer stage, New York, New York.
FTL Design Engineering Studio

Carlos Moseley Music Pavilion, front view, New York, New York.
FTL Design Engineering Studio.

TENTS AND TEMPORARY STRUCTURES 115

Mushroom-shaped pavilion at Expo 2002, distant view, Neuchatel, Switzerland.
Architect: Sbriglio / Multipack. Canobbio and M. Matteo Piazza

Mushroom-shaped pavilion at Expo 2002, waterfront view.
Architect: Sbriglio / Multipack. Canobbio and M. Matteo Piazza

116   FABRIC ARCHITECTURE

Mobile tent for the Pope, 2003.
Covertex GmbH

Mobile tent for the Pope, 2006.
Covertex GmbH

TENTS AND TEMPORARY STRUCTURES 117

AT&T Global Village at night during the Olympics, Atlanta, Georgia. FTL Design Engineering Studio

AT&T Global Village with projected images during the Olympics. FTL Design Engineering Studio

118   FABRIC ARCHITECTURE

National Symphony Orchestra bandstand, Washington, DC.
FTL Design Engineering Studio

Tent for Costa Rican presidential event, San José, Costa Rica.
Samuel J. Armijos

TENTS AND TEMPORARY STRUCTURES 119

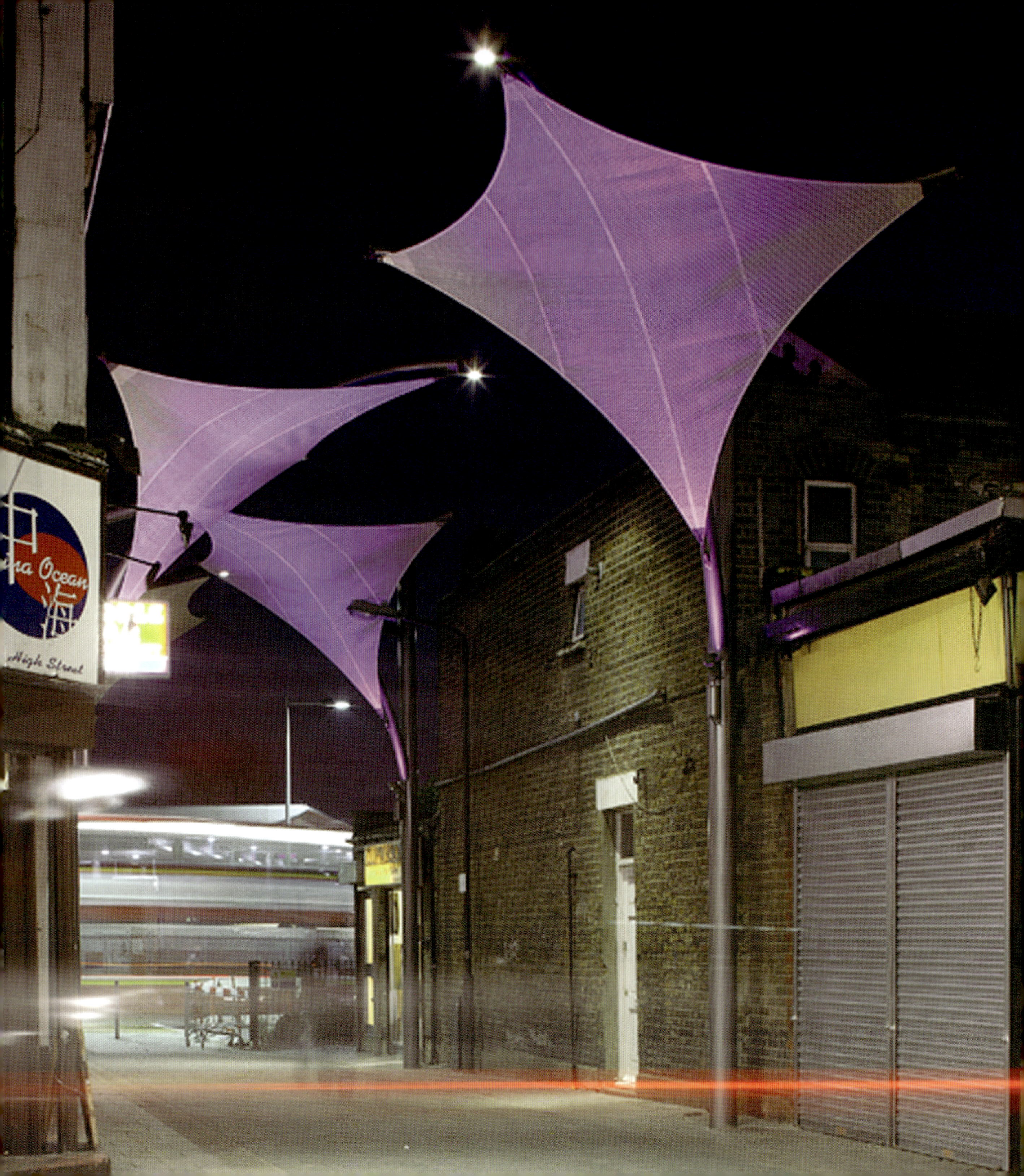

na Ocean
High Street

5

SHADE STRUCTURES

A shade structure is an awning, canopy, tent, or tensioned fabric structure designed to provide ultraviolet (UV) protection with a degree of transparency. Today, an increasing number of fabric structures are being designed exclusively to provide shade, especially in outdoor dining areas, playgrounds and parks, and places of public assembly, where it is advisable to limit people's exposure to direct sunlight.

Shade structures are made with materials designed to breathe, resist tearing, and be stable under tension. The amount of UV protection can vary from 70 to 90 percent depending on the openness of the fabric structure. Shade structures not only provide UV protection but also shelter from hail, wind, and water, depending on the fabric chosen.

Shade structures may be fixed or movable and can have graphics applied or projected on to them as well.

Attaching shade structures to or over a window or curtain wall reduces direct solar gain on a building. Freestanding shade structures keep equipment from getting too hot, protect people and objects against hail damage, and can help in reducing the amount of evaporation in pools and fountains (see top image, page 123). They are useful for screening mechanical and construction equipment from view.

Shade structure over playground, Lundigan Park, Burbank, California. Shade Structures

Shade structures, Centennial Hills Park, aerial view, Las Vegas, Nevada. Sunports

Centennial Hills Park shade structures, detail. Sunports

Detail of a lifeguard stand. Sunports

Three point sail over waterpark. Sunports

SHADE STRUCTURES 123

Darling Tennis Center, aerial view, Las Vegas, Nevada. Sunports

Detail of shade structures, Darling Tennis Center. Sunports

Shade structures, Classic HUMMER dealership, Grapevine, Texas. Sunports

"Being" by G. H. Bruce. G. H. Bruce

Hypar rooftop shade structure, New York, New York. G. H. Bruce

SHADE STRUCTURES 125

Wave shade structures, Southdown Park, Pearland, Texas. Sunports

Multiple shade structures, Camp Pendleton, California. Shade Structures

Shade structures with stone cladding at base. Sunports

Multi-panel polygon shade structure over playground. Sunports

Slant hip shade structure over bleacher. Sunports

SHADE STRUCTURES 127

"Sky Bridge" by G. H. Bruce.

G. H. Bruce

Custom shade structures, Dallas Zoo, Dallas, Texas. Sunports

128 FABRIC ARCHITECTURE

Hypar shade structures over a swimming pool. Sunports

Multiple shade structures at a water park facility. Sunports

SHADE STRUCTURES 129

Covered parking garage, Navona condominium, Naples, Florida. Sunmaster of Naples

Shade structure at community pool, Sacramento, California. Shade Structures

130   FABRIC ARCHITECTURE

Custom tensioned shade structure, Grimes Park, Desoto, Texas. Sunports

Community pool shade. G. H. Bruce

SHADE STRUCTURES 131

(above left) "Tsunami" shade structures. G. H. Bruce

(above right) Fabric structures in urban setting, United Kingdom. Fabric Architecture

Shade structures, Oakridge Mall, San Jose, California. Fabritec Structures

Bleacher shade canopies at McFalls Park, Grand Prairie, Texas. Sunports

Shade structures, Magma Ranch. Scottsdale, Arizona. Shade Structures

SHADE STRUCTURES 133

Multi-panel shade structure.
Shade Structures

Great America food court at night,
Santa Clara, California.
Fabritec Structures

134   FABRIC ARCHITECTURE

Multiple shade structures at theme park. Sunports

Shade structure on deck of private residence. Miro Rivera Architects

SHADE STRUCTURES 135

A series of multipanel shade structures. Shade Structures

Shade structure over daycare playground, Northern California.
Shade Structures

Multi-hypars on urban plaza. Sunports

Three-point sail at waterpark. Sunports

"Lotus Flower." G. H. Bruce

Port cochere at Las Vegas Premium Outlets. Fabritec Structures

Superspan hip shade structure over playground. Sunports

Shade structure, Children's Discovery Museum, Rancho Mirage, California. Fabritec Structures

SHADE STRUCTURES 139

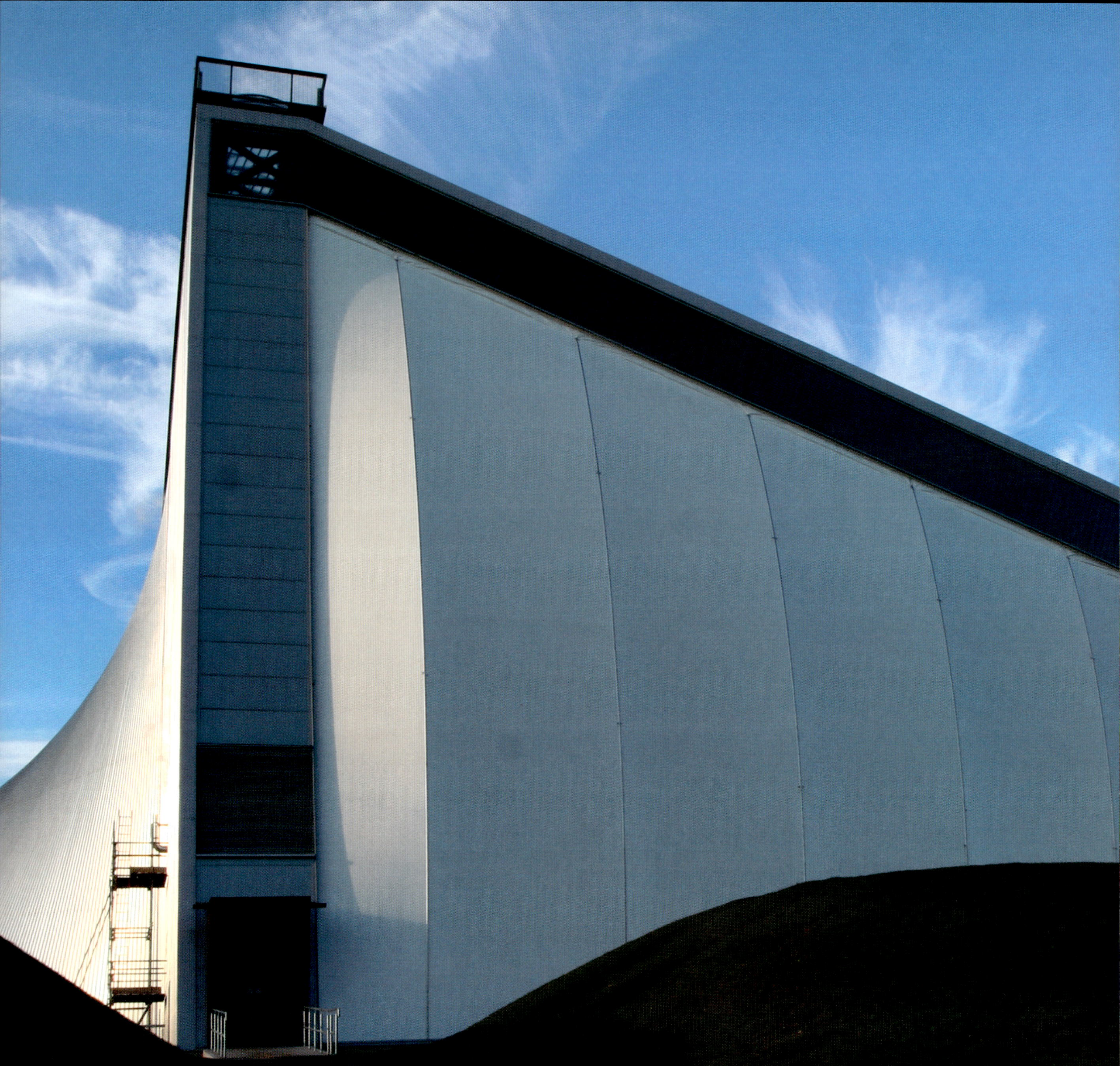

6
TEXTILE FAÇADES

Textile façades—screens used on the exterior of buildings—are a relatively new category of fabric architecture, though in the form of awnings, banners, and billboards they are familiar uses of fabric in a vertical orientation. However, improved printing technology, longer-lasting materials, and the pressing need to reduce the amount of energy consumed by buildings are making textile façades ever more appealing on the exterior of both old and newly constructed commercial, industrial, public, and residential buildings. Textile façades can be quickly and simply erected. They reduce heat gain not only within the building, but on its surface as well.

Textile façades normally are constructed of mesh fabric, which, unlike interior blinds and building overhangs, allows a view out while reducing energy consumption and increasing solar protection. Façades can be installed as one membrane or in configurations of multiple membranes. Large membranes require a supporting structure to protect them from wind deflection and vibration; cables, struts, and outriggers stabilize multiple configurations.

Given a blank surface on which to print or project images and patterns, owners are "branding" buildings, selling space on the façade and finding creative ways to promote their building, product, or services. And textile facades are no longer only vertical; they increasingly take on more three-dimensional and organic shapes (see top image, page 146).

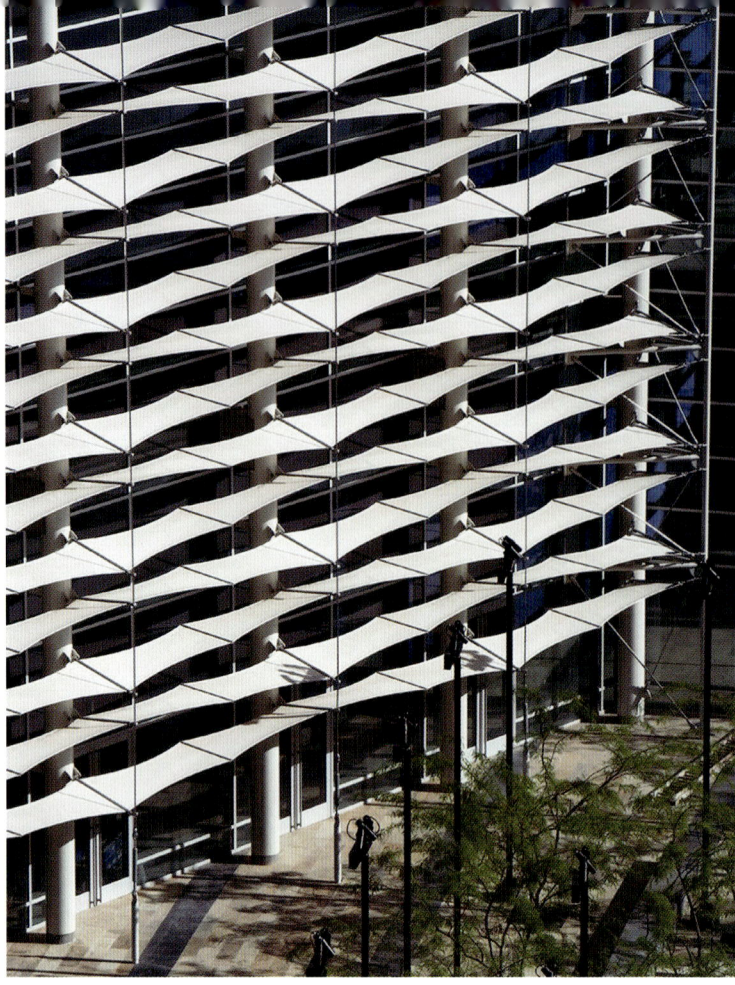

Exterior shading device, Mesa Arts Center, Mesa, Arizona.
Architects: BOORA Architects. FTL Design Engineering Studio

Detail of shade system, Mesa Arts Center. Architects: BOORA Architects. FTL Design Engineering Studio

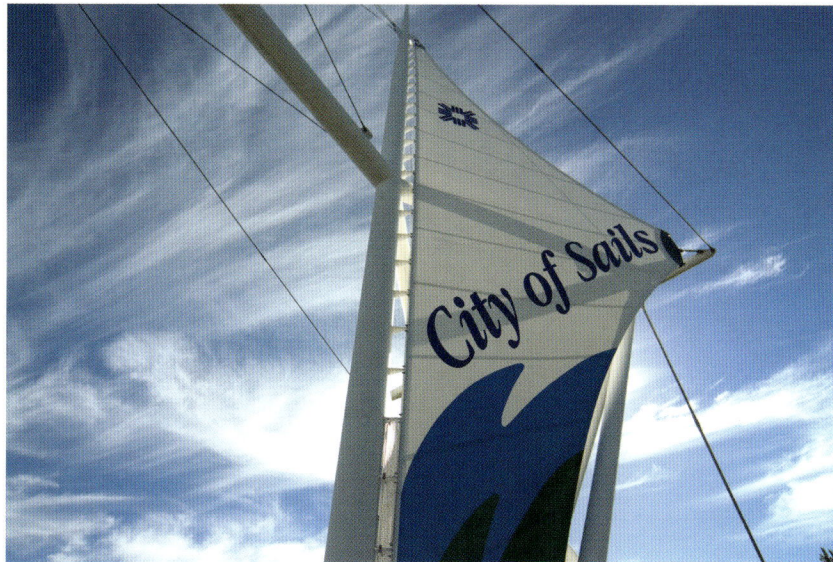

Textile façade, Philadelphia Park Casino, Philadelphia, Pennsylvania. Architects: Daroff Design. Daroff Design

Airport entrance façade, Auckland, New Zealand. Structurflex

Textile façade, Silverspur Office, Rolling Hills Estate, California. X-Ten Architecture. Ferrari Textiles

TEXTILE FAÇADES

Textile façade, Yendi building, Bulle, Switzerland. Ferrari Textiles

Textile façade, Cheney Stadium, Tacoma, Washington. Rainier Industries

RAF Museum, Cosford, Shropshire, United Kingdom.
Design by Base Structures, Ltd.
Ferrari Textiles

Textile façade, Migros Distribution Center at night, Suhr, Switzerland.
Ferrari Textiles

TEXTILE FAÇADES 145

LA Farmers Market at night, Los Angeles, California. Architects: House & Robertson. Fabritec Structures

Bleacher banner with ski jump image for the Winter Olympics, Salt Lake City, Utah. Rainier Industries

Fin-shaped beacon, Holiday Inn, Washington, D.C.
WDG Architecture. Fabritec Structures

Dynaform for BMW, Frankfurt, Germany.
Franken Architekten

TEXTILE FAÇADES 147

Custom fabric structure, Kaleidoscope Mall, Mission Viejo, California. Architects Altoon Porter. Fabritec Structures

(opposite) Detail of exterior sun shade, Phoenix Library at night, Phoenix, Arizona. Architects: Will Bruder + Partners, Ltd. FTL Design Engineering Studio

Façade of Phoenix Library, Phoenix, Arizona. Architect: Will Bruder + Partners. FTL Design Engineering Studio

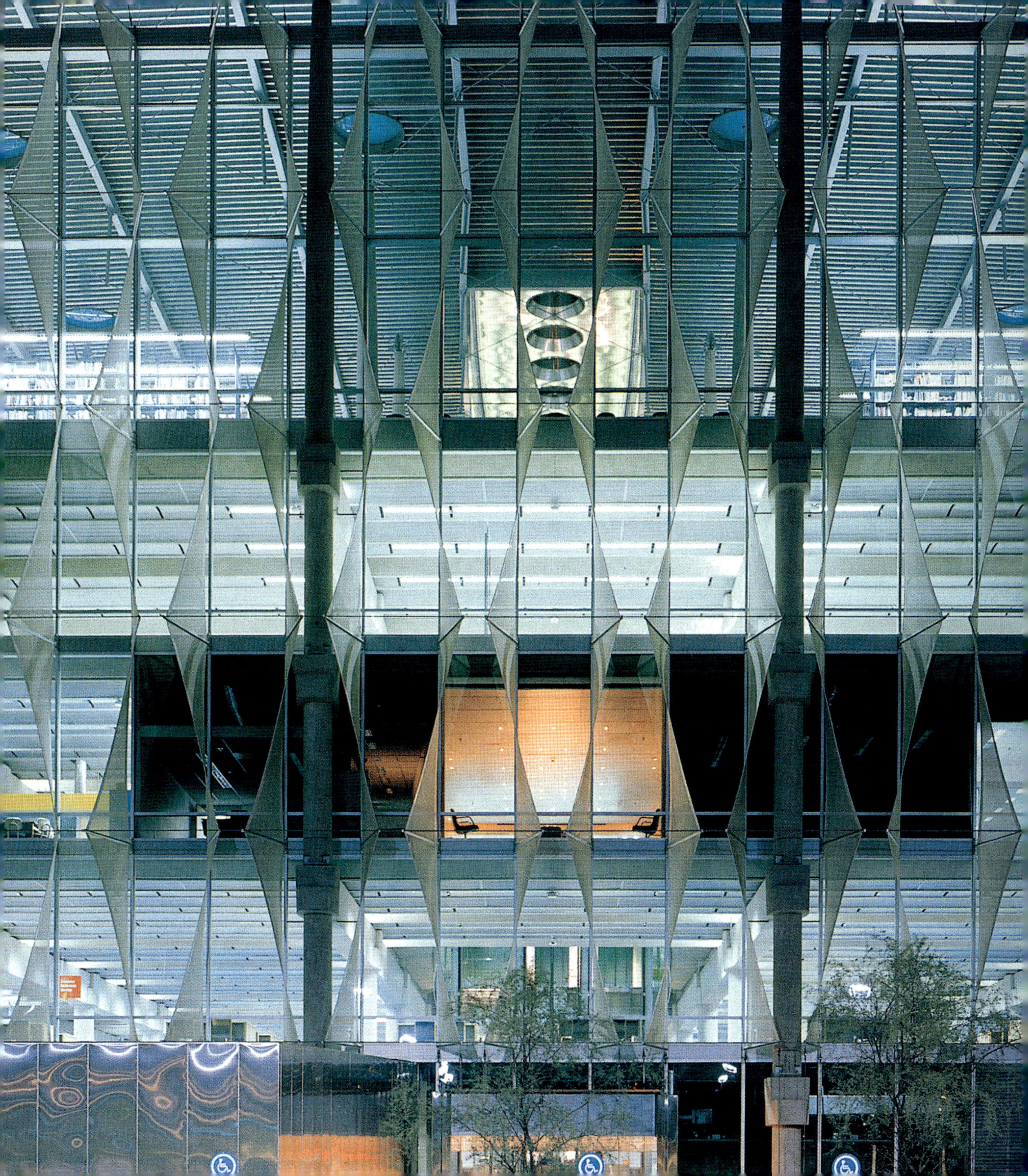

Miroiterie Flon Textile Façade, Lausanne, Switzerland. Hightexworld

Detail of shade structure, Arizona State University Food Court, Tempe, Arizona. Rainier Industries

Entry, Arizona State University Food Court. Rainier Industries

TEXTILE FAÇADES 151

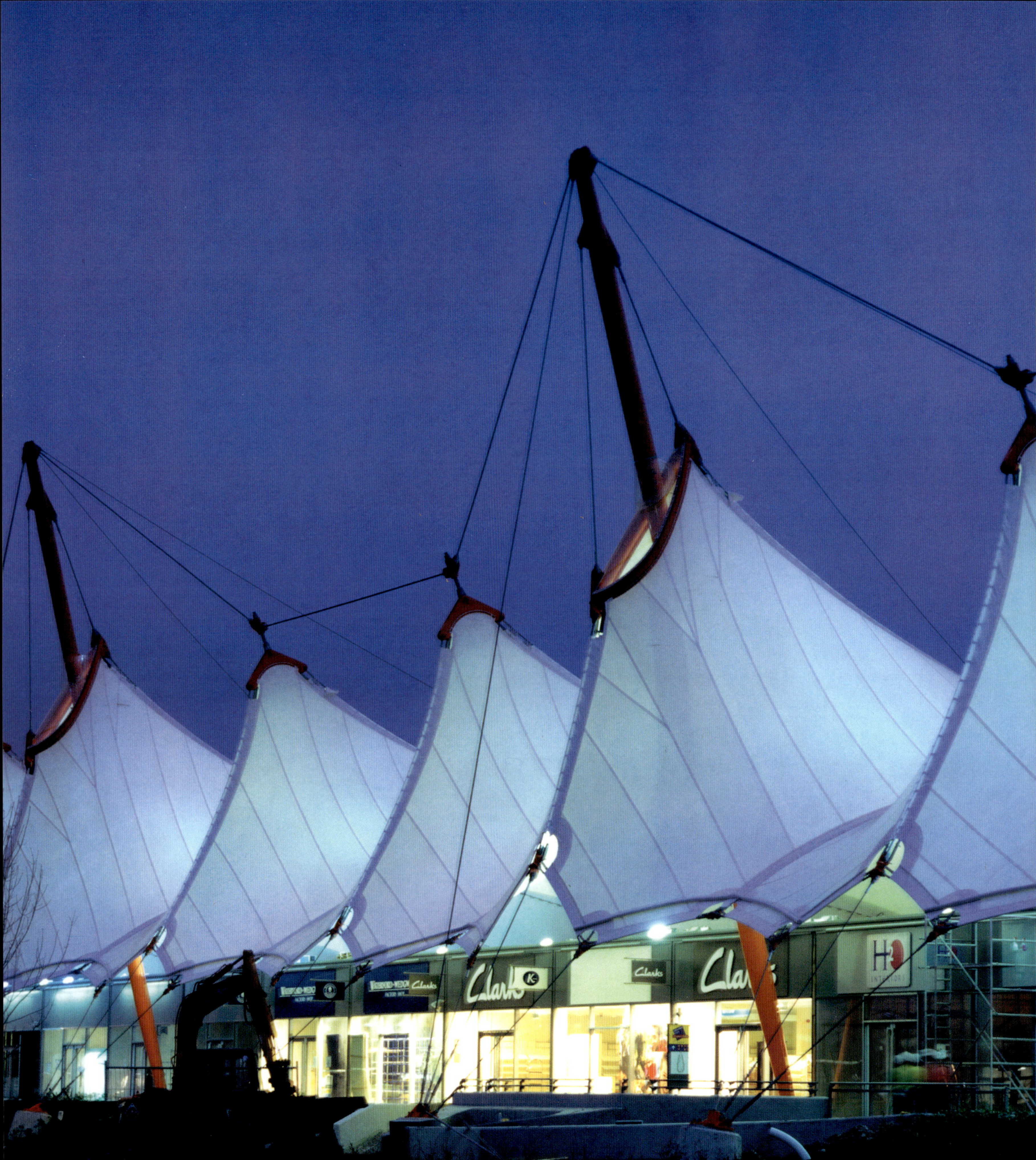
Clarks

7

MAST-SUPPORTED STRUCTURES

Mast-supported structures are membranes of one or multiple peaks supported by interior and perimeter masts or adjacent buildings. They require the least amount of structural material to construct. A bale ring, which is used to raise large membranes, or a solid steel top plate, which is used to support smaller membranes, connects the fabric to the interior masts, while perimeter masts support the fabric by means of membrane plates, which join the membrane and catenary cables. These perimeter masts are designed either as fixed connections at the base, which means they can be quite large and require a large foundation, or pin-connected, which allows for movement and results in smaller masts and foundations. A pin-connected mast requires tiedowns for stability. Some mast-supported structures do not have perimeter masts but rely instead on outriggers or structural members that cantilever off central masts, much like an umbrella.

The peaks of a mast-supported structure can vary in shape and size depending on the overall design, method of attachment, and structure under load. They tend to have round, oval, or elliptical openings, which may be covered or left open. The membrane is normally patterned with seams radiating from the top of the opening. These triangular panels require more complex patterning and more seams than nonradiating patterned structures. They are also less efficient in the utilization of fabric, which is manufactured in long rectangular rolls. For small-scale projects and structures with multiple panels, seam orientation can be planned to optimize material use.

Most mast-supported structures rely on the fabric's structural characteristic without the need for additional support, but as the structures get larger, radial cables are required and precautionary safety cables may be installed above the membrane from mast to mast and to the ground (see top image, page 166). In the event the membrane fails, the cables keep the mast erect.

Las Vegas Premium Outlet Mall, distant view, Las Vegas, Nevada. Adams Hennon Architects. Fabritec Structures

Las Vegas Premium Outlet Mall, close up view. Adams Hennon Architects. Fabritec Structures

Las Vegas Premium Outlet Mall at night. Adams Hennon Architects. Fabritec Structures

Las Vegas Premium Outlet Mall, showing highly reflective ceiling. Adams Hennon Architects. Fabritec Structures

MAST-SUPPORTED STRUCTURES 155

156 FABRIC ARCHITECTURE

(opposite top) **Royal Melbourne Showgrounds at night, Melbourne, Australia.** Structurflex

(opposite bottom) **Royal Melbourne Showgrounds at dusk.** Structurflex

Detail of top, Royal Melbourne Showgrounds. Structurflex

Mast detail, Royal Melbourne Showgrounds. Structurflex

MAST-SUPPORTED STRUCTURES

Multiple units, Abu Dhabi Corniche, United Arab Emirates. Structurflex

Single unit, Abu Dhabi Corniche. Structurflex

Mesa Arts Center trees at night, Mesa, Arizona.
FTL Design Engineering Studio

(below left) Mesa Arts Center trees, evening view.
FTL Design Engineering Studio

(below right) Custom tension structure, Chandlers Wharf, Liverpool, United Kingdom.
Fabric Architecture

MAST-SUPPORTED STRUCTURES 159

Passenger Ferry Terminal, Warnemuen, Germany. Covertex GmbH

Passenger Ferry Terminal bale ring detail. Covertex GmbH

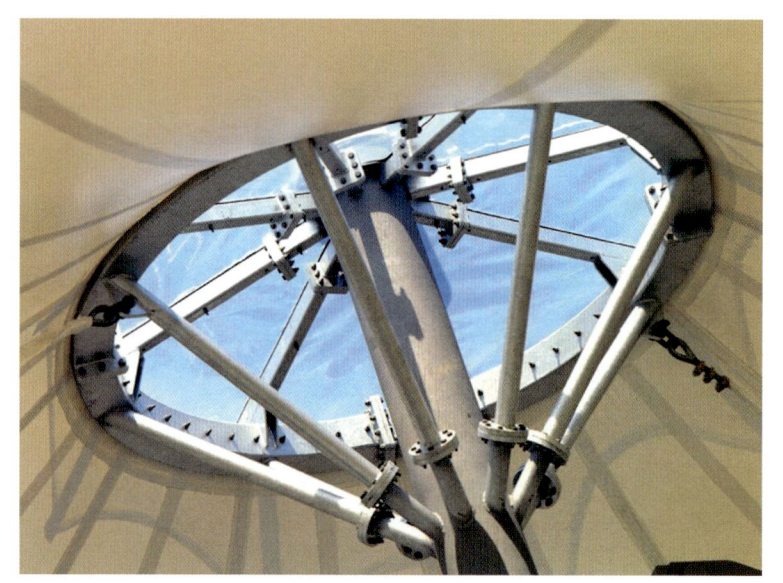

Hudson River Park Pavilion, New York, New York. Fabritec Structures

Thomas Moore College Pavilion, view from above, Longton, United Kingdom.
Fabric Architecture

Thomas Moore College Pavilion, cone detail.
Fabric Architecture

MAST-SUPPORTED STRUCTURES 161

High-rise membrane structure detail with oculus, Osijek, Croatia. Covertex GmbH

Detail, Cogi Farms, Pawling, New York. Fabritec Structures

(opposite) **Flying mast detail.** J. J. Carter

162   FABRIC ARCHITECTURE

MAST-SUPPORTED STRUCTURES 163

Thousand Islands Lake. Fabrimax

Canopy on shooting range, Bisley, United Kingdom. Fibertech

Fabric structure, HEB Supermarket, Harlington, Texas. Fabritec Structures

Detail of roof structure at shopping mall, Kirchberg, Luxenbourg. Cenotec

Whitehaven Pavilion, United Kingdom. JJ Carter

MAST-SUPPORTED STRUCTURES 165

Fabric structure, Outlet Village Retail, Ashford, United Kingdom.

Richard Rogers Partnership Architects. Architen Landrell

Western view of World Cup stadium, Seoul, Korea. Geiger Engineers

Custom tension fabric structure, Kuwait Airport, Kuwait. Fibertech

Entry, Fahd Stadium, Riyadh, Saudi Arabia. Geiger Engineers

MAST-SUPPORTED STRUCTURES 167

Al Hamra Oasis Sports Center, Riyadh, Saudi Arabia. Fibertech

(below) Porirua Mall, view from below, Wellington, New Zealand. Structurflex

(opposite) Porirua Mall at night. Structurflex

168 FABRIC ARCHITECTURE

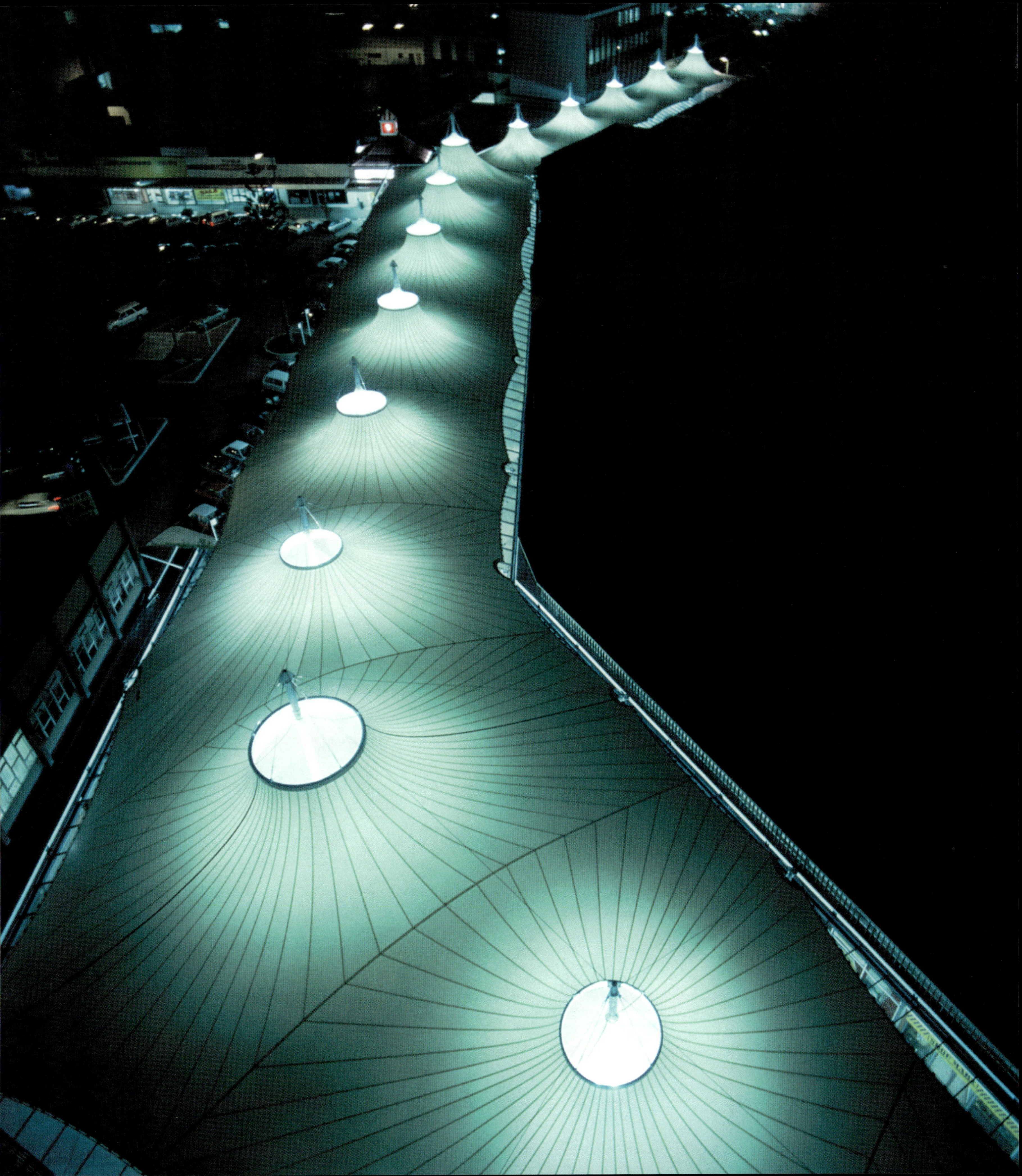

Pier 6 Music Pavilion, Baltimore, Maryland. FTL Design Engineering Studio.

Custom tension structure, Stazio complex, Boulder, Colorado. Samuel J. Armijos.

Membrane plate detail, Hampton Convention Center, Hampton, Virginia. **FTL Design Engineering Studio**

Shaoxing Ke Bridge at night, Shaoxing, China. **Fabrimax**

MAST-SUPPORTED STRUCTURES   171

(above left) **Imagination Building, London, United Kingdom.** Architect: Ron Herron. Architen Landrell

(above right) **Glyndebourne Opera House, Sussex, United Kingdom.** Hopkins Architects. Architen Landrell

Multi-cone walkway canopies, Mid-Peninsula Day School, Palo Alto, California. Fabritec Structures

Flying mast canopies, Dalton Park Shopping Mall, Murton, United Kingdom. Architen Landrell

Dalton Park Shopping Mall structure.
Architen Landrell

MAST-SUPPORTED STRUCTURES 173

(top left) **Two-cone pavilion, Caesars Palace at night, Las Vegas, Nevada.** GSB Architects. Fabritec Structures

(middle left) **Caesars Palace Food Pavilion.** GSB Architects. Fabritec Structures

(bottom left) **Single-cone pavilion, Caesars Palace at night.** GSB Architects. Fabritec Structures

Persimmons Home Quayside Housing Development, United Kingdom. Fabric Architecture

174   FABRIC ARCHITECTURE

Challenge Petrol Stations at night, throughout New Zealand. Structurflex

Grandstand for TSV, Gersthofen, Germany. Cenotec

MAST-SUPPORTED STRUCTURES 175

Celebration Park pavilion, Allen, Texas. Sunports

Nautica Amphitheater by day, Cleveland, Ohio. Geiger Engineers

Nautica Amphitheater at night. Geiger Engineers

MAST-SUPPORTED STRUCTURES 177

San Diego Convention Center at night, San Diego, California. DeNardis Engineering

Detail of flying mast at San Diego Convention Center. DeNardis Engineering

Tensioned fabric structure, Carras Park, Missoula, Montana. Rainier Industries

Hampton Convention Center, side view, Hampton, Virginia.
FTL Design Engineering Studio

Hampton Convention Center at night. FTL Design Engineering Studio

MAST-SUPPORTED STRUCTURES 179

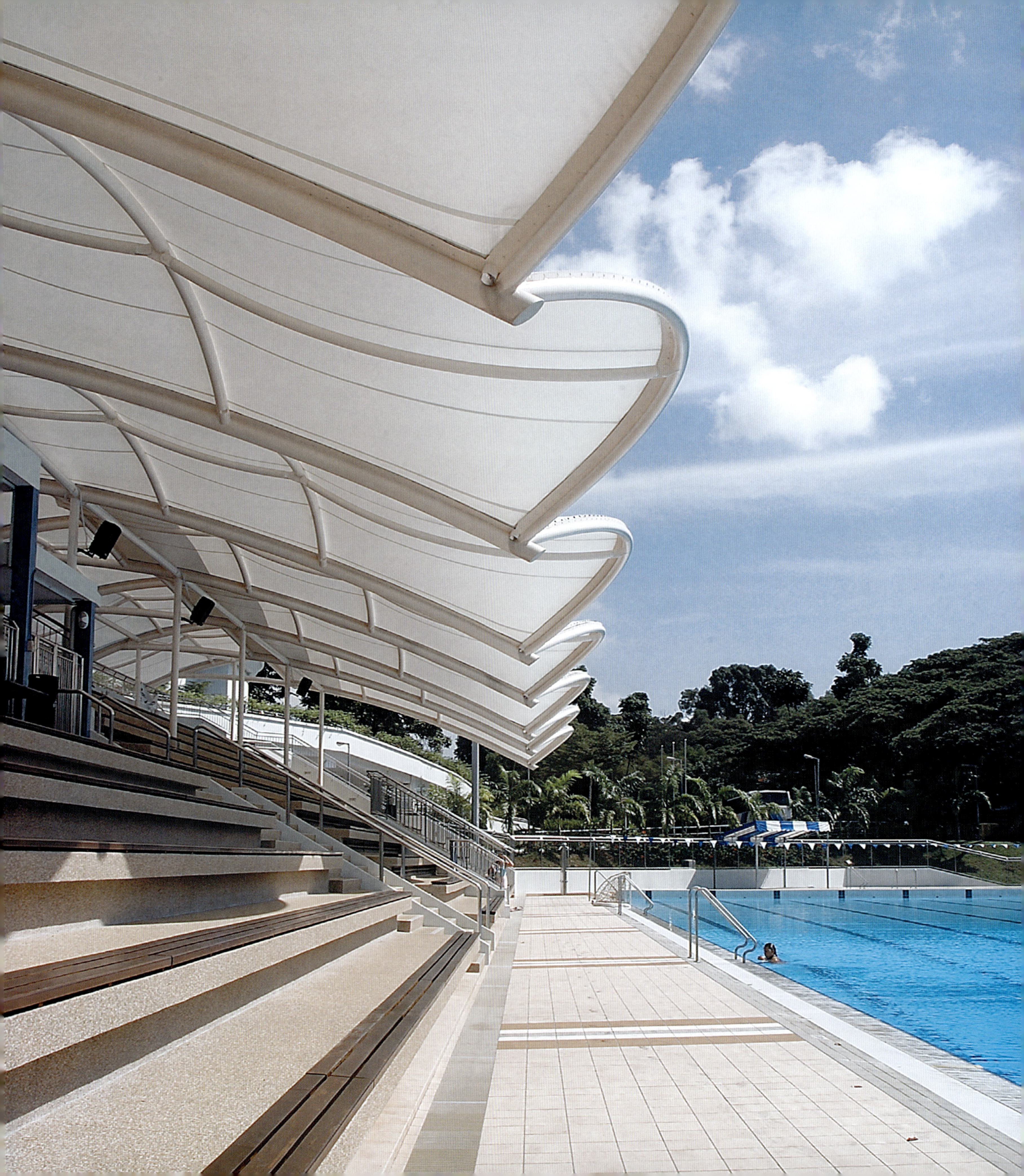

8

ARCH- AND FRAME-SUPPORTED STRUCTURES

Arch-supported structures are barrel-like in form and need no interior supports because their curved compression members provide the main supporting element. Typical arch-supported designs include barrel vaults, which have arches parallel to each other, and fan vaults, whose arches radiate from a central point. Cross arches or diagonal bracing is often used to give lateral stability.

The arch may be made of steel, aluminum, concrete, composites, a laminated wooden beam, or a multichord truss. It is important that the top surface be smooth so the material can slide or move over it. The membrane does not necessarily have to sit on top of the arch for support, however: it can be supported by hanging from points on the underside of the structural member (see bottom image, page 185).

Frame-supported structures are essentially very large awnings, commonly used when high lateral loads are not desirable, as in the case of a pre-existing building or land with poor soil conditions. The primary structural components carry the majority of forces within the system, so the fabric is purely cladding. Space frames—lightweight structures constructed from interlocking struts in a geometric pattern—and custom steel skeleton frames that do not have double curvature are common examples of frame-supported structures in which the fabric is fitted and attached directly to the frame.

Vitrashop entry at night.

Architen Landrell

Vitrashop front entry.

Architen Landrell

182 FABRIC ARCHITECTURE

Fabric structure, Bard College, Annandale-on-Hudson, New York.
Architects: Ashokan Architecture.
Fabritec Structures

Shopping mall aerial view, Xanadu, Madrid, Spain. Fibertech

Xanadu shopping mall at night. Fibertech

ARCH- AND FRAME-SUPPORTED STRUCTURES 183

Noble House at night, Great Barrier Island, New Zealand. Structurflex

Tensioned fabric structure, Cribbs Causeway, Bristol, United Kingdom. Architects: Richard Hemmingway & Partners. Architen Landrell

Charlottesville Amphitheater, Charlottesville, Virginia.
FTL Design and Engineering Studio

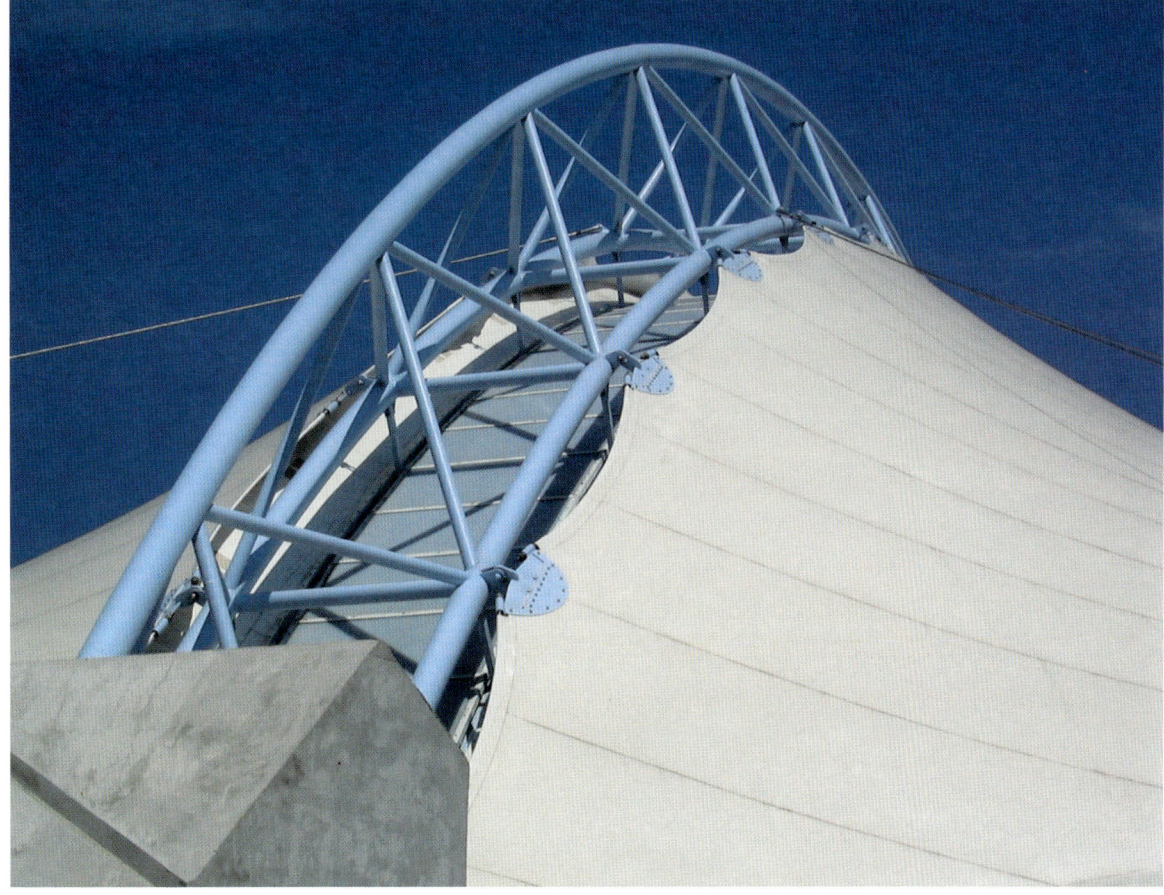

Detail of arch and membrane, Chatham Maritime, Kent, United Kingdom. Architen Landrell

ARCH- AND FRAME-SUPPORTED STRUCTURES 185

Gerland Stadium, Lyon, France. Ferrari Textiles

Froettmaning U-Bahn Station, Munich, Germany.
Covertex GmbH

Carrefour Shopping Mall, Riyadh, Saudi Arabia. Fibertech

ARCH- AND FRAME-SUPPORTED STRUCTURES

Walkway, Saddleback Community Church, Mission Viejo, California.
Fabritec Structures

Bangkok Airport interior, Bangkok, Thailand.
Hightexworld

188   FABRIC ARCHITECTURE

Day view of LiteHouseOne Oasis building. LiteHouseOne and Hightexworld

Night view of LiteHouseOne Oasis building. LiteHouseOne and Hightexworld

ARCH- AND FRAME-SUPPORTED STRUCTURES 189

Hertz canopies, Oklahoma Airport, Tulsa, Oklahoma. Ferrari Textiles

Cantilever walkway system, American Canyon, California. Fabritec Structures

190   FABRIC ARCHITECTURE

Footbridge, view from below, Auckland, New Zealand. Structurflex

Viaduct footbridge. Structurflex

192   FABRIC ARCHITECTURE

(opposite) **Plashet Unity Bridge, aerial view, London, United Kingdom.** Architen Landrell

Plashet Unity Bridge interior. Architen Landrell

Dome stadium, University of Northern Iowa, aerial view, Cedar Falls, Iowa. DeNardis Engineering

Dome stadium, University of Northern Iowa, interior. DeNardis Engineering

ARCH- AND FRAME-SUPPORTED STRUCTURES 193

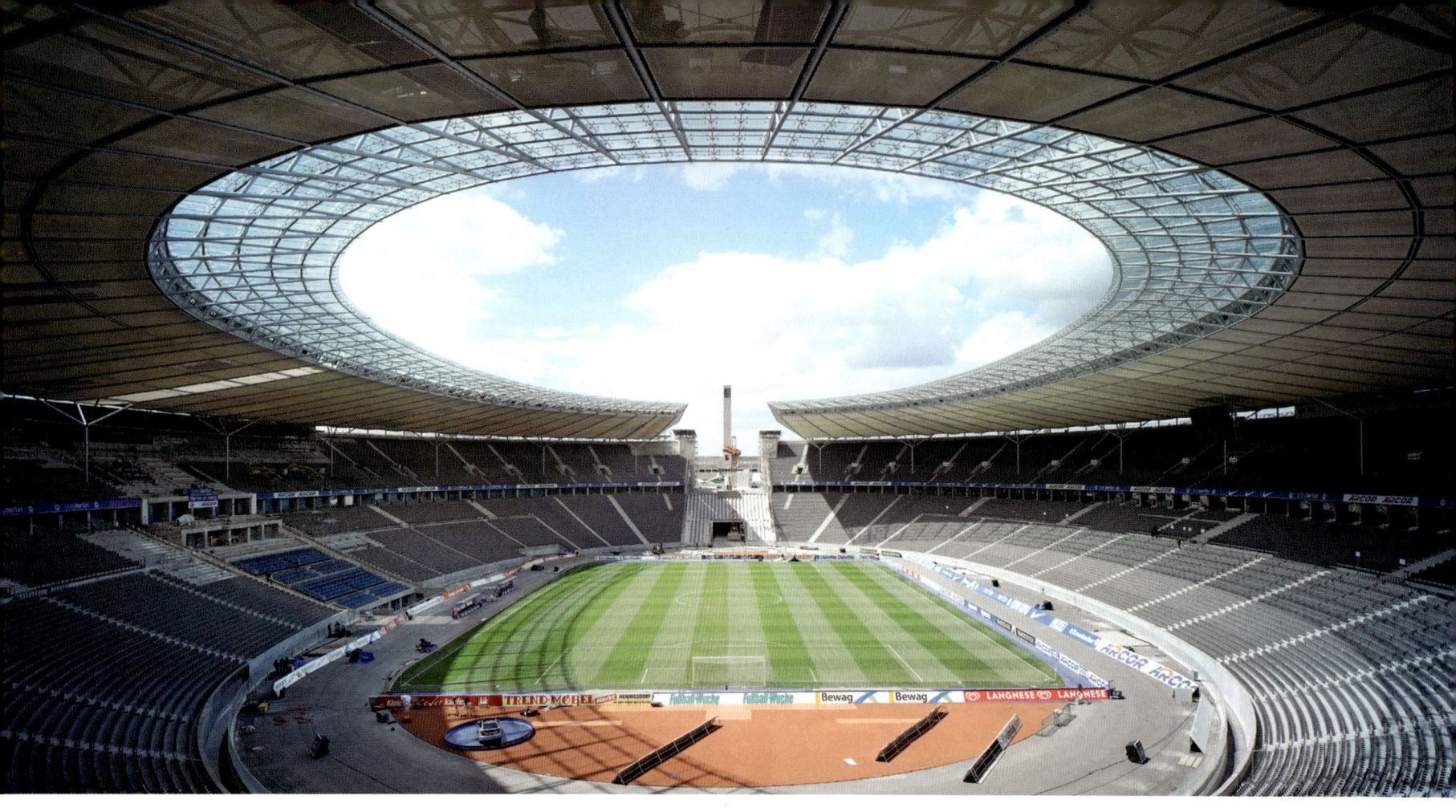

Olympic Stadium, Berlin, Germany. Hightexworld

Interior view showing liner of Olympic Stadium. Hightexworld

Edmonton Green Station, night view, Edmonton, United Kingdom. Architen Landrell

Edmonton Green Station, day view. Architen Landrell

Grandstand canopy, Princeton University track, Princeton, New Jersey. Samuel J. Armijos

ARCH- AND FRAME-SUPPORTED STRUCTURES 195

Island entrance canopy, Mainau, Germany. Cenotec

Nanjing Toll Station, day view, Nanjing, China. Fibertech

196 FABRIC ARCHITECTURE

Bus station, Parnell Place, night view, Cork, Ireland. J. J. Carter

Bus station, Parnell Place, day view. J. J. Carter

ARCH- AND FRAME-SUPPORTED STRUCTURES 197

Detail of O2 Riverwalk canopy in purple, London, United Kingdom. Architen Landrell

O2 Riverwalk canopy. Architen Landrell

(opposite) O2 Riverwalk canopy at night. Architen Landrell

ARCH- AND FRAME-SUPPORTED STRUCTURES   199

AT&T Pavilion at night, Olympic Games, Atlanta, Georgia. FTL Design Engineering Studio

Yam O Railway Station, Hong Kong. Fibertech

Las Vegas Motor Speedway Neon Garage, Las Vegas, Nevada.
Fabritec Structures

Auckland Netball complex interior, Auckland, New Zealand.
Structurflex

Auckland Netball complex exterior. Structurflex

ARCH- AND FRAME-SUPPORTED STRUCTURES 201

Stadium, Foshan, China. Engineers: Schlaich Bergermann and Partners. Ferrari Textiles

Al Wasamiya fuel station, Bahrain. Fibertech

Detail of gangway at Port Imperial Ferry Terminal, Weehawken, New Jersey. Structurflex

Port Imperial Ferry Terminal from above. Structurflex

Port Imperial Ferry Terminal overlooking New York City. Structurflex

ARCH- AND FRAME-SUPPORTED STRUCTURES 203

Auckland Tennis Centre, Auckland, New Zealand. Structurflex

Water treatment plant exterior, Valenton, France. Ferrari Textiles

204   FABRIC ARCHITECTURE

Water treatment plant interior. Ferrari Textiles

ARCH- AND FRAME-SUPPORTED STRUCTURES 205

(top) **United World College pool, Singapore.** Structurflex

(above) **United World College pool, view from below.** Structurflex

(left) **United World College pool, long view.** Structurflex

(opposite) **Custom fabric structure, Sainsbury's Marsh Mills Superstore, Plymouth, United Kingdom.** Architen Landrell

ARCH- AND FRAME-SUPPORTED STRUCTURES 207

Membrane structure, Ascot Racecourse, Ascot, United Kingdom. Hightexworld

Covered parking structure, Research Park, Austin, Texas. Sunports

208 FABRIC ARCHITECTURE

Papageno Children's Theatre, Frankfurt, Germany. Covertex GmbH

Departure and arrival entrance canopies, Love Field, Dallas, Texas. Fabritec Structures

ARCH- AND FRAME-SUPPORTED STRUCTURES 209

Matiatia Wharf terminal, Waiheke Island, New Zealand. Structurflex

Matiatia Wharf waterfront. Structurflex

Charlotte Bandshell,
Charlotte, North Carolina.
Samuel J. Armijos

Membrane roof structure, British Racing Drivers Club,
Silverstone, United Kingdom. Architen Landrell

ARCH- AND FRAME-SUPPORTED STRUCTURES 211

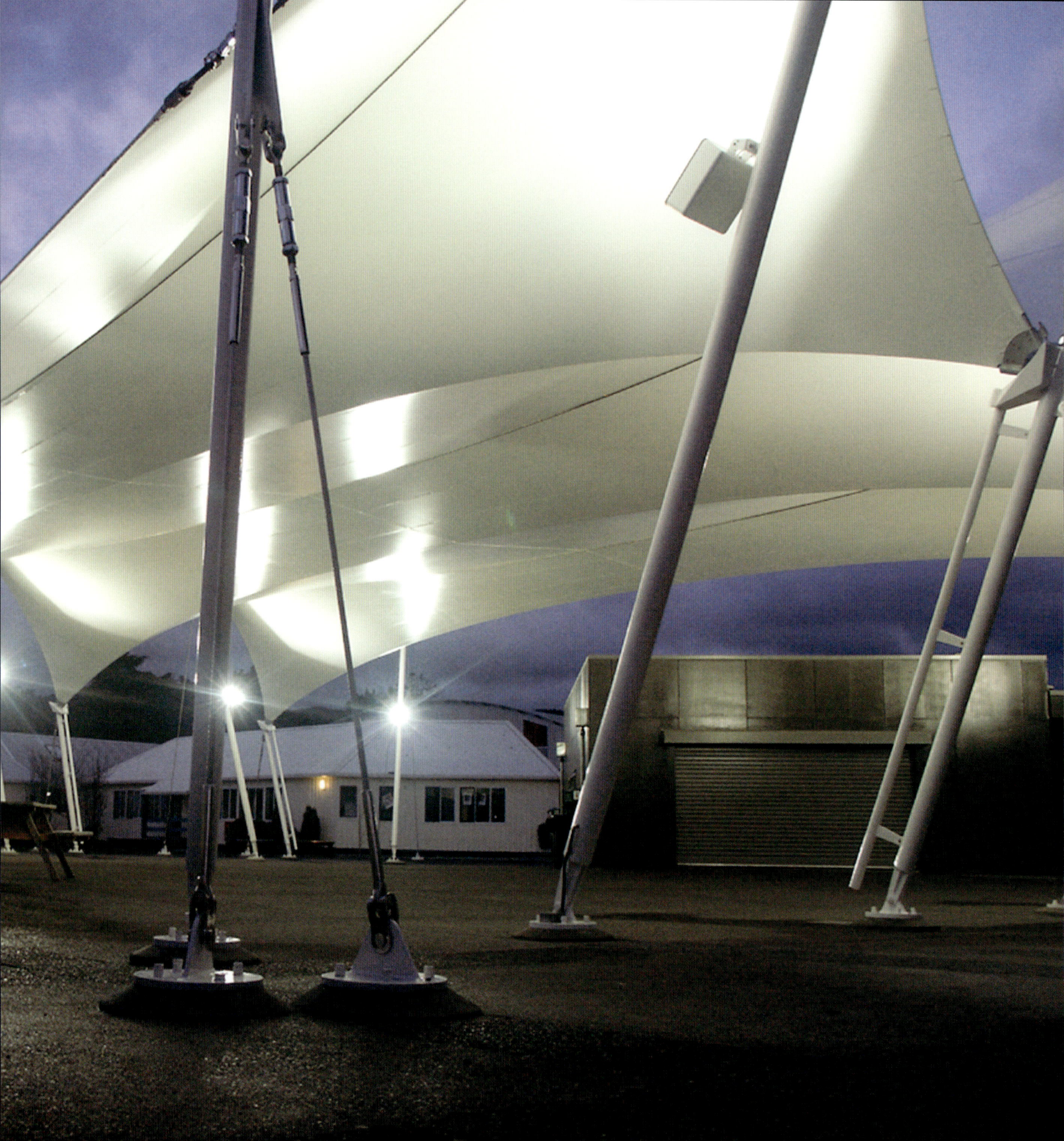

9

POINT-SUPPORTED STRUCTURES

Point-supported structures are forms with a minimum of four points of attachment, with either straight or curved edges that produce a clear span with no center mast. The classic point-supported structure is the saddle shape or hypar.

Point-supported structures may take a variety of shapes, depending on the number of anchor points and the position of the supporting elements; however, double curvature is essential. Several point-supported structures can be combined if they share a common mast. The membrane can also be supported from above at specific points by cables or rods coming off the perimeter masts or high points on a building. Point-supported structures may be designed as repeated modular units and in combination with mast-supported or arch-supported structures to create unique and large spaces.

A point-supported clear span may also be created by supporting the membrane along its perimeter with a row of masts. In this case, ridge cables that carry gravity loads hang much like a suspension bridge between masts while valley cables, which resist uplift forces, form an arch halfway between the next rows of masts. The perimeter masts are held by safety and tie down cables. Arranging the masts in linear fashion results in a series of alternating high and low points along the perimeter. When the masts are arranged in a radial pattern, a star-shaped structure with either a low or high center results.

18th and Vine Music Pavilion, Kansas City, Missouri. Fabritec Structures

Entrance to Queen Elizabeth Hospital, Woolwich, United Kingdom.
Architen Landrell

Pavilion, Oswego Lake, Oregon. Fabritec Structures

Three peaks of Al Shatee Mall fabric structures, rooftop view, Dammam, Saudi Arabia. Fibertech

Al Shatee Mall interior. Fibertech

Four peaks of Al Shatee Mall fabric structures, rooftop view. Fibertech

POINT-SUPPORTED STRUCTURES 215

Entry, VMF Market, Al Ain, United Arab Emirates. Structurflex

VFB club entry, Stuttgart, Germany. Hightexworld

216   FABRIC ARCHITECTURE

Membrane plate detail, Las Vegas Premium Outlet Mall, Las Vegas, Nevada. Fabritec Structures

Hampshire Rose Bowl grandstand, Southampton, United Kingdom. Architects: Hopkins Architects. Architen Landrell

POINT-SUPPORTED STRUCTURES 217

Nokia covered parking, distant view, White Plains, New York. Fabritec Structures

Edge detail, Nokia covered parking structure. Fabritec Structures

Entry, Nokia covered parking structure. Fabritec Structures

Gutter detail, Nokia covered parking structure. Fabritec Structures

POINT-SUPPORTED STRUCTURES

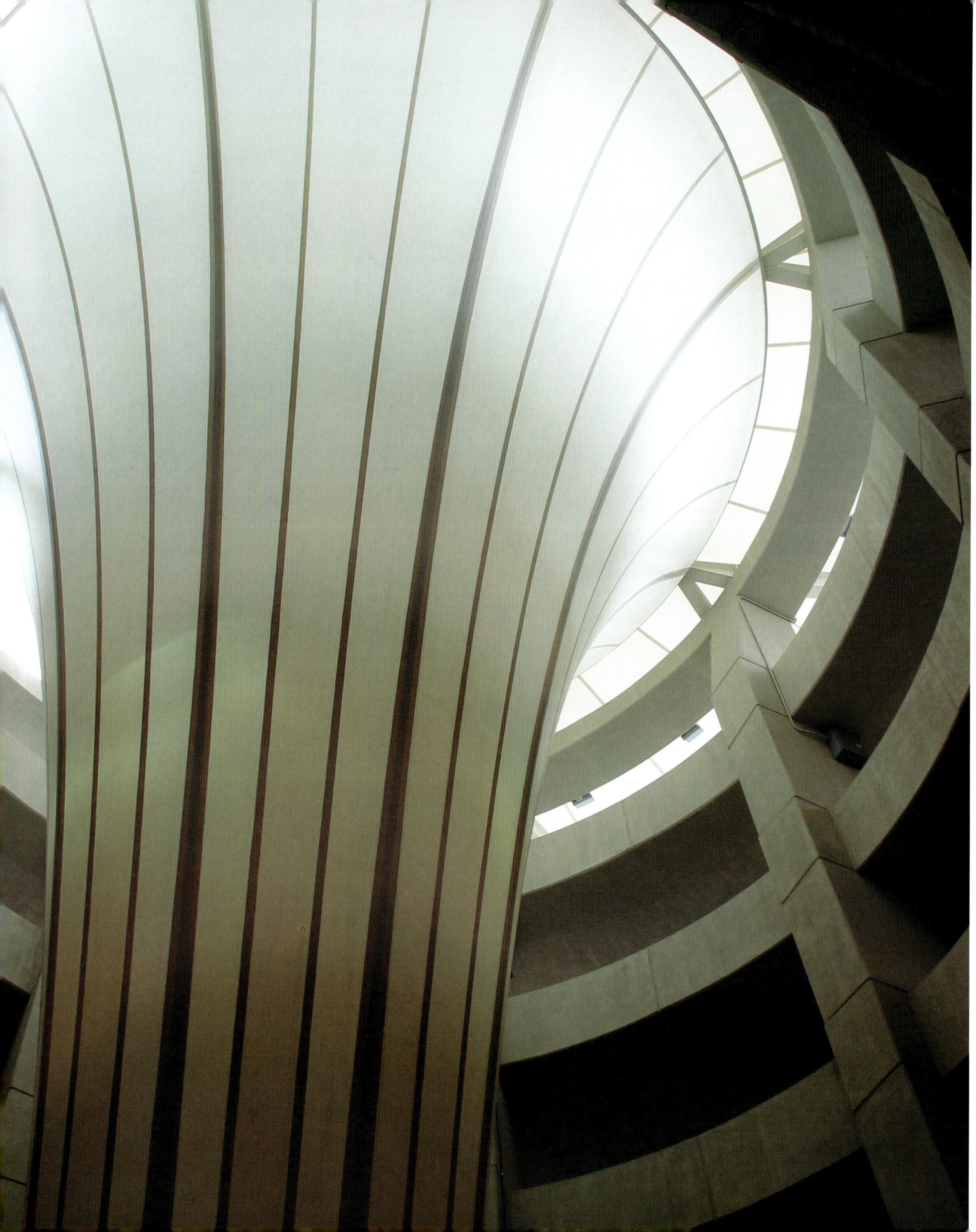

(opposite) **Helix fabric structure, airport parking garage, Raleigh-Durham, North Carolina.**
Geiger Engineers

Legoland theme park canopy, Carlsbad, California. Fabritec Structures

Millennium Park walkway, Kent, Michigan.
Fabritec Structures

POINT-SUPPORTED STRUCTURES

Palm Springs Airport, view from above, Palms Springs, California. *DeNardis Engineers*

Palm Springs Airport, view from below. *DeNardis Engineers*

Inland Revenue Centre, Nottingham, United Kingdom. Hopkins Architects.
Hightexworld

Membrane roof, Piazza Italia, Milan, Italy.
Naizil

POINT-SUPPORTED STRUCTURES 223

Walkway, Embassy of Finland, Washington, DC. Heikkinen-Komonen Architects. FTL Design Engineering Studio

Canada Place waterfront at night, Vancouver, British Columbia. Geiger Engineers

Canada Place by day. Geiger Engineers

POINT-SUPPORTED STRUCTURES 225

Private residence boat dock canopy, Lake Austin, Texas.
Miro Rivera Architects

Cirque de Soleil building, Orlando, Florida.
Architect: Rockwell Group. FTL Design Engineering Studio

226   FABRIC ARCHITECTURE

Outdoor classroom and play area, Cotham School, Bristol, United Kingdom. Architen Landrell

Cynthia Woods Mitchell Center for the Performing Arts, Woodlands, Texas. Design: Horst Berger Partners. DeNardis Engineers

Fabric structure for an urban marketplace, Zeltweg, Austria. Covertex GmbH

Marina Mall exterior, Damman, Saudi Arabia.
Fibertech

Marina Mall interior.
Fibertech

POINT-SUPPORTED STRUCTURES

Vodafone entry structure, Newbury, United Kingdom. Architen Landrell

Train station at Leipzig Airport, Leipzig, Germany. Cenotec

230   FABRIC ARCHITECTURE

Bird's-eye view of train station at Leipzig Airport, Leipzig, Germany. Cenotec

Platform view of train station at Leipzig Airport, Leipzig, Germany. Cenotec

POINT-SUPPORTED STRUCTURES 231

Fabric structure, Hutt International Boys School, view from above, Wellington, New Zealand. Structurflex

Fabric structure, Hutt International Boys School, at night, view from below. Structurflex

Mast and tiedown detail, Hutt International Boys School. Structurflex

Highway tollbooth, Songjiang, China. Fabrimax

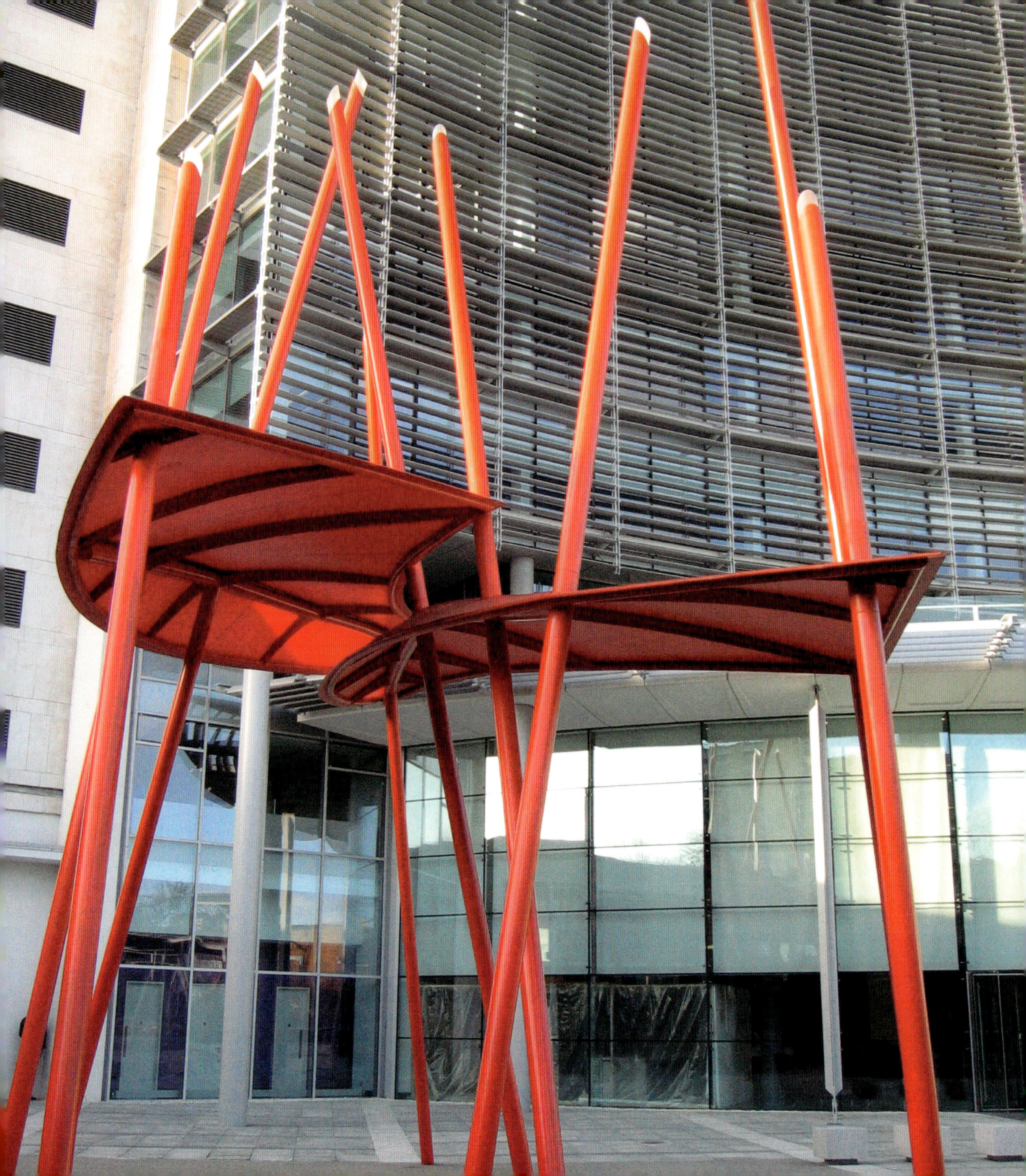

10
FUTURE STRUCTURES

Fabric architecture continues to evolve, due to advances in technology and materials and changing decorative and structural needs. Interior applications and textile façade projects have shown us that fabric structures need not always have double curvature and catenary edges.

We have also seen that fabrics can span greater distances than glass, and be supported by very light structural members. ETFE (ethylenetetrafluorethylene) cushions can be molded into a variety of shapes and sizes, and provide innovative, cost-effective, and lightweight cladding. ETFE foils are already being used as an alternative to structural glass in atriums, greenhouses, swimming pools, and water-park enclosures.

Pneumatic structures such as air halls, tennis bubbles, and inflatables have a long history as forms that use air for support. They continue to provide an economical and creative way to enclose large spaces. The idea of using air in combination with high-strength fabric has encouraged innovative design and engineering approaches for new building types. Air-inflated structures that erect themselves in place, high-pressure air beams that can support snow loads, and air ships used for transport cargo are no longer only theoretical concepts.

Photovoltaic (PV) thin-film technology has also shown promise of being used in tensioned fabric structures. These thin films convert light energy into electrical energy. PV technology in fabric structures is presently used in the military; commercial applications will arrive sooner rather than later in areas needing shade, shelter, and electricity (see upper left image, page 251).

Sustainability and green design, and compliance with such rating systems as Leadership in Energy and Environmental Design (LEED), are big issues in architecture today. Fabric structures are finding their place in projects requiring natural daylight, energy savings, and reduced reliance on fossil fuels. Multilayer fabric structures filled with a variety of materials to add thermal and acoustical benefits without losing natural daylight are being used in promising ways. Structures made with sustainable products are particularly appealing; recycled PVC and fabrics with longer life spans are certainly steps in the right direction towards a green architecture.

The following illustrations present a look at some classic air structures as well as recent buildings and new concepts that will certainly become reality in the not-too-distant future.

Dyson traveling air structure at night, New York, New York.
FTL Design Engineering Studio and EventQuest

Rosa Parks Bus Station, Detroit, Michigan. FTL Design Engineering Studio

Sky Song, Arizona State University, west view, Tempe, Arizona. FTL Design Engineering Studio

FUTURE STRUCTURES 237

Retractable roof closed, HVB Bank, Munich, Germany. Gore

(below left) Retractable roof, view from below, HVB Bank. Gore

(below right) Detail of retractable roof, HVB Bank. Gore

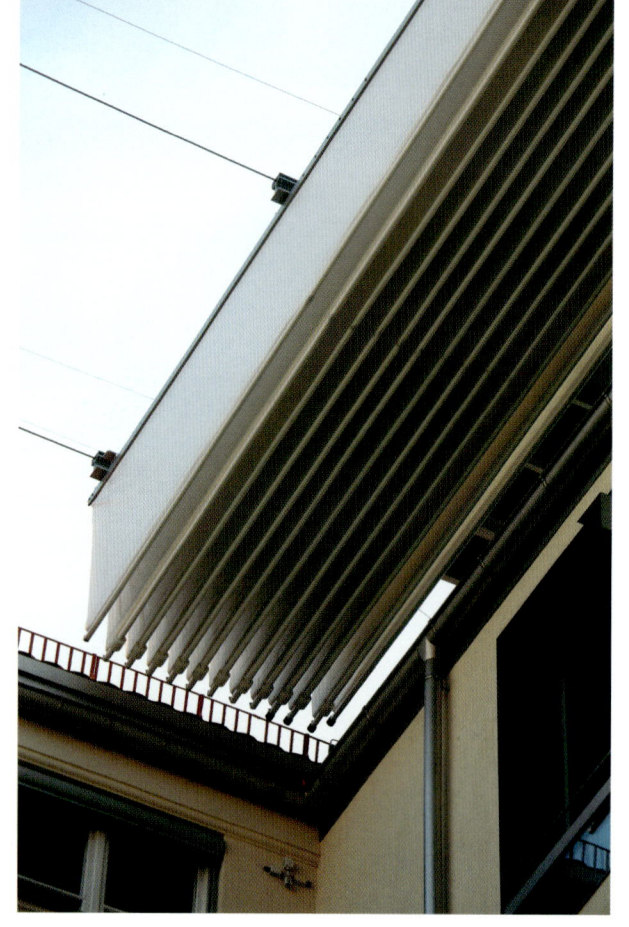

Dynaform pavilion for BMW, under construction, Frankfurt, Germany.
Covertex GmbH

ETFE structure, exterior, Alnwick Garden, Alnwick, United Kingdom.
Hopkins Architects. Hightexworld

ETFE structure, interior, Alnwick Garden. Hopkins Architects. Hightexworld

Prienavera Pool, aerial view, Chiemsee, Germany. Hightexworld

Prienavera Pool, interior detail. Hightexworld

ETFE skylight at yacht club, Nansei, Japan. Hightexworld

Concept for Reno Ice Skating Rink. Fabritec Structures

FUTURE STRUCTURES

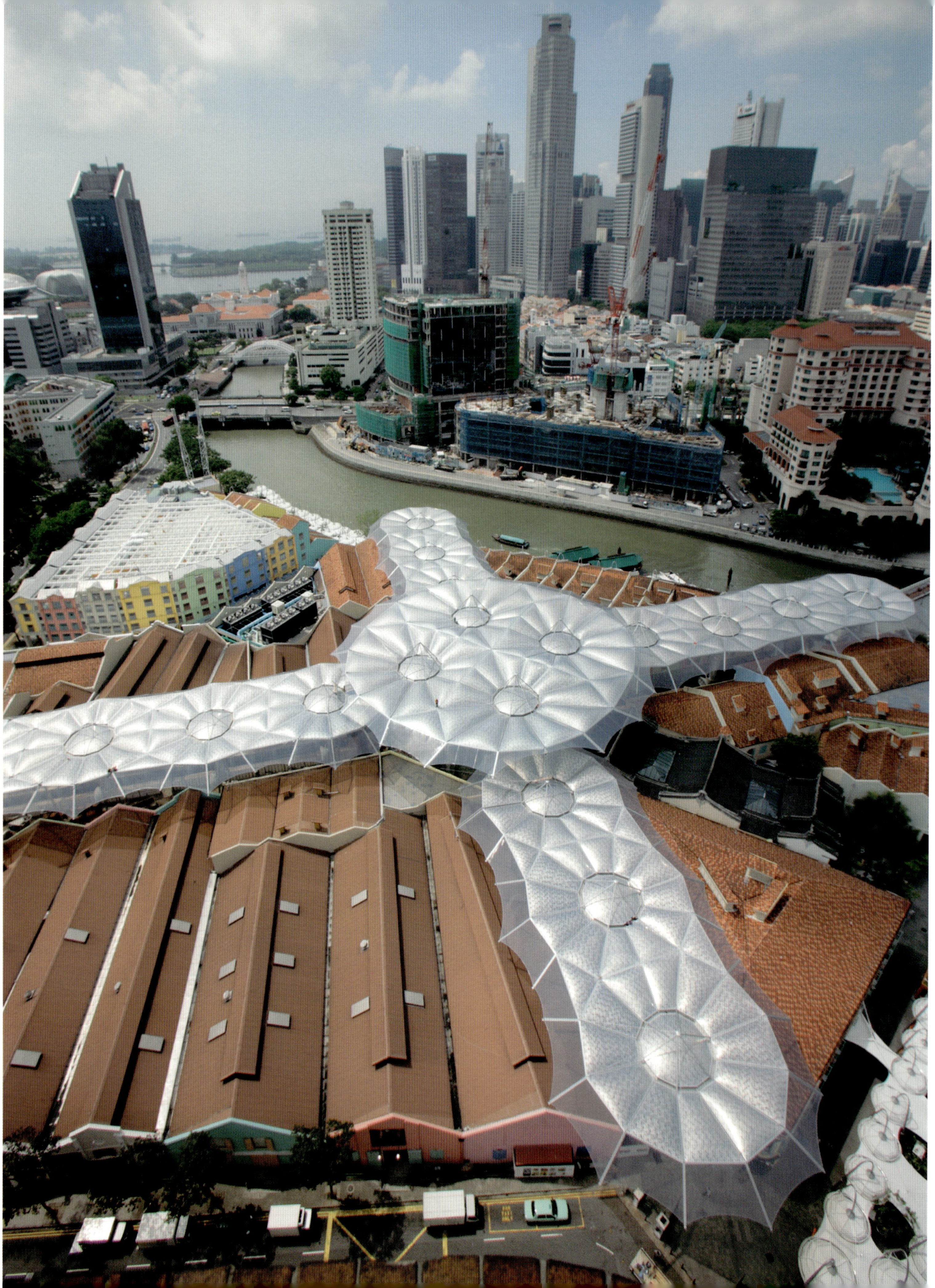

(opposite) **Clarke Quay shopping mall, aerial view, Singapore.** Allsop Architects. Hightexworld

Clarke Quay shopping mall, view from above. Allsop Architects. Hightexworld

Clarke Quay shopping mall, view from below. Allsop Architects. Hightexworld

FUTURE STRUCTURES 243

National Space Centre, Leicester, United Kingdom. Architects: Nicholas Grimshaw and Partners. Hightexworld

244   FABRIC ARCHITECTURE

Side view, Tubaloon Performance Shelter, Kongsberg, Norway. Architects: SNØHETTA. Canobbio

Front view, Tubaloon Performance Shelter, Kongsberg, Norway. Architects: SNØHETTA. Canobbio

Montreaux covered parking structure at night, view from above. Designers: Tensairity concept by Airlight. PD Interglas

FUTURE STRUCTURES 245

Tensairity covered parking structure from below, Montreaux, Switzerland. Design: Airlight, Ltd. PD Interglas

Tensairity covered parking structure with colored lighting. Design: Airlight, Ltd. PD Interglas

Tensairity covered parking structure membrane detail.
Design: Airlight, Ltd. PD Interglass

Concept for Eco-cabin.
FTL Design Engineering Studio

FUTURE STRUCTURES 247

Retractable roof, aerial view, Castle Kufstein, Kufstein, Austria. Gore

Retractable roof closed, view from below, Castle Kufstein. Gore

Retractable roof closing, Castle Kirstein.
Gore

Retractable roof closed, Castle Kufstein.
Gore

FUTURE STRUCTURES 249

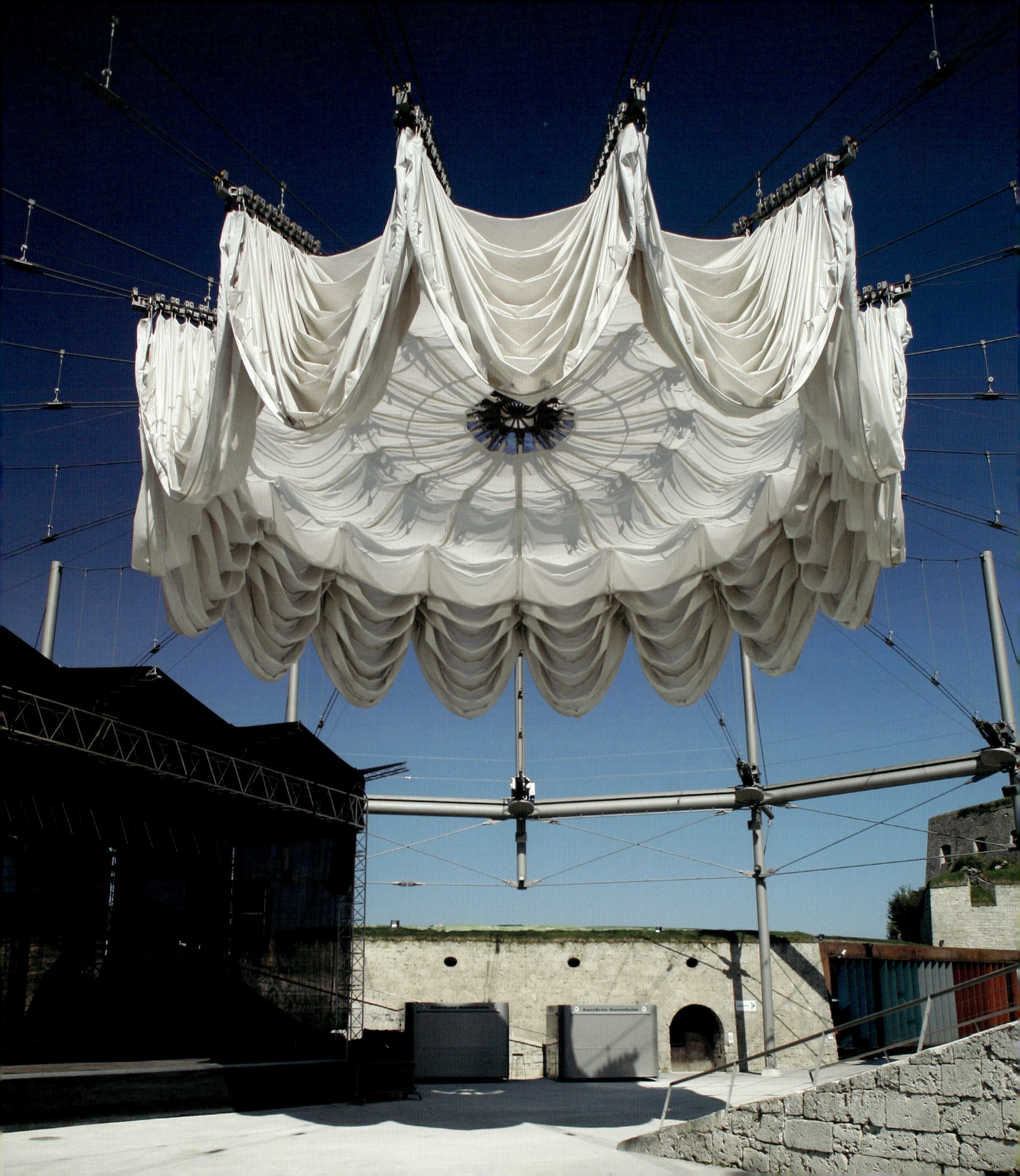

Concept for photovoltaic covered parking. Fabritec Structures

(opposite) Retractable roof open, Castle Kufstein. Gore

Structure using photovoltaic cells, "Under the Sun" exhibit, Cooper Hewitt Museum, New York, New York. FTL Design Engineering Studio

Photovoltaic parking structure rendering for New York State Energy Research and Development Authority. FTL Design Engineering Studio

FUTURE STRUCTURES 251

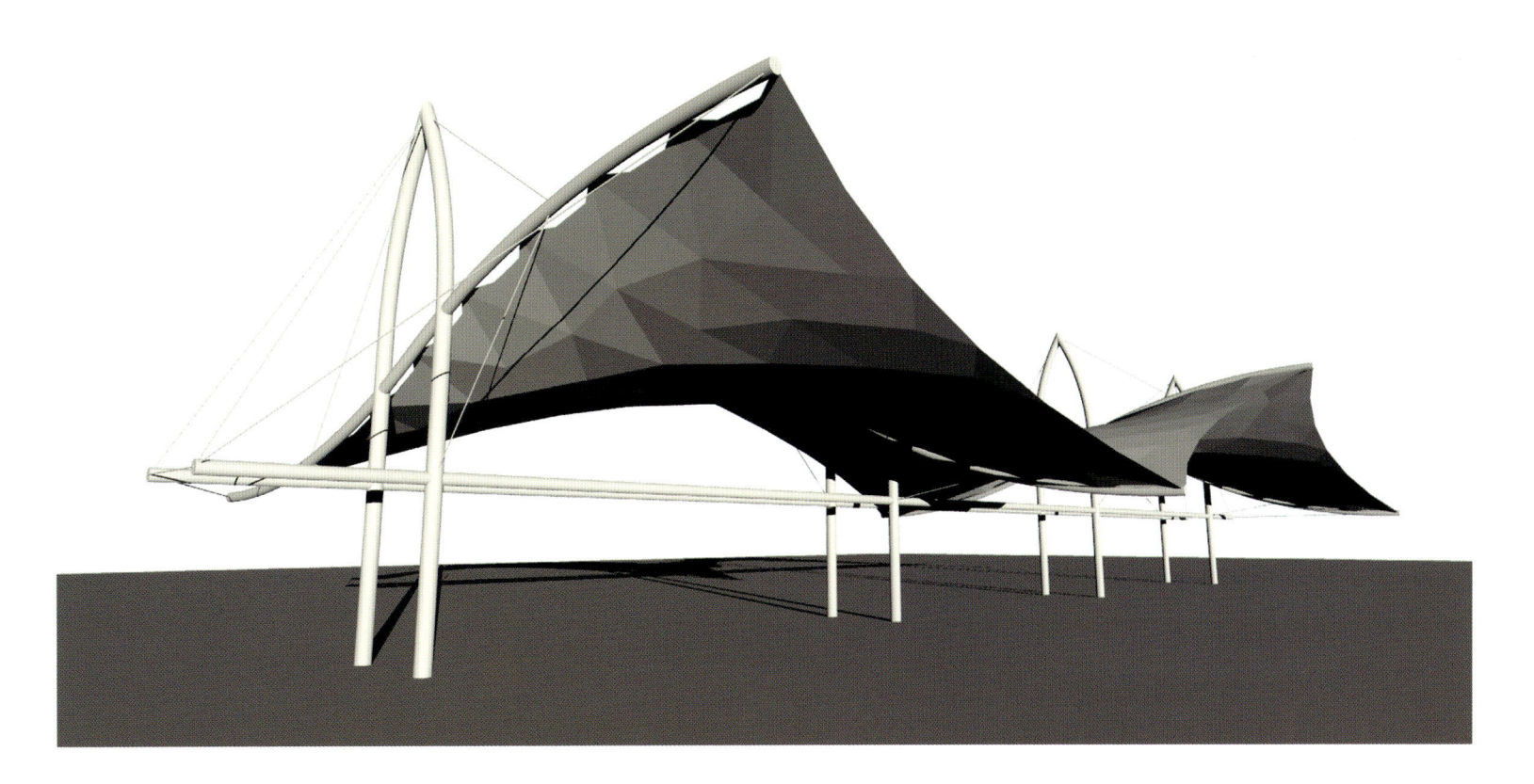

Skykitten Air Cargo ship, Oxford, United Kingdom. Tensys

(below left) Diana Edmunds Empress sculpture, London, United Kingdom. Architen Landrell

(below right) Concept for fabric skyscraper. FTL Design Engineering Studio

Waterfront fabric structure rendering. Fabritec Structures

Fabric ceiling panel at the Worrell, Weeks and Walcott Stand at Kensington Oval, Barbados. Architen Landrell

FUTURE STRUCTURES 253

Sun Valley Amphitheater concept, summer, Sun Valley, Idaho. FTL Design Engineering Studio

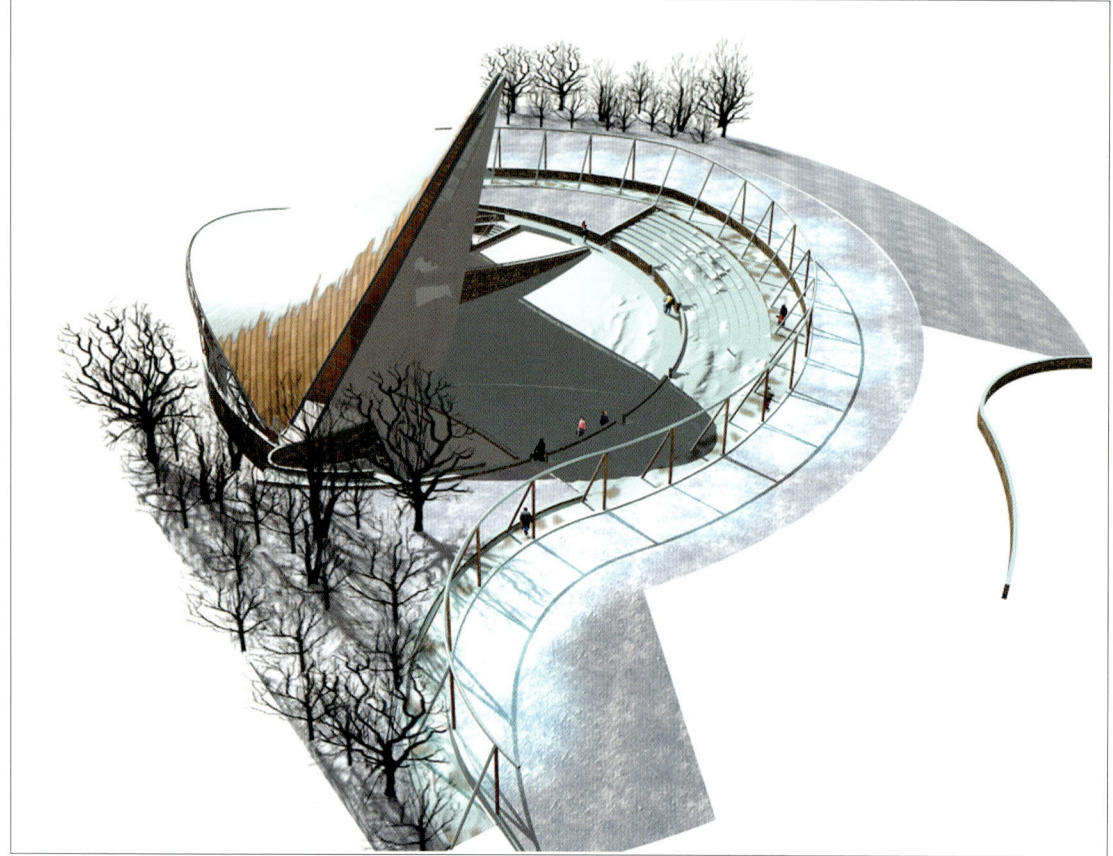

Sun Valley Amphitheater concept, winter. FTL Design Engineering Studio

Anish Kapoor's *Marsyas*, Tate Modern, London, United Kingdom. Hightexworld

FUTURE STRUCTURES 255

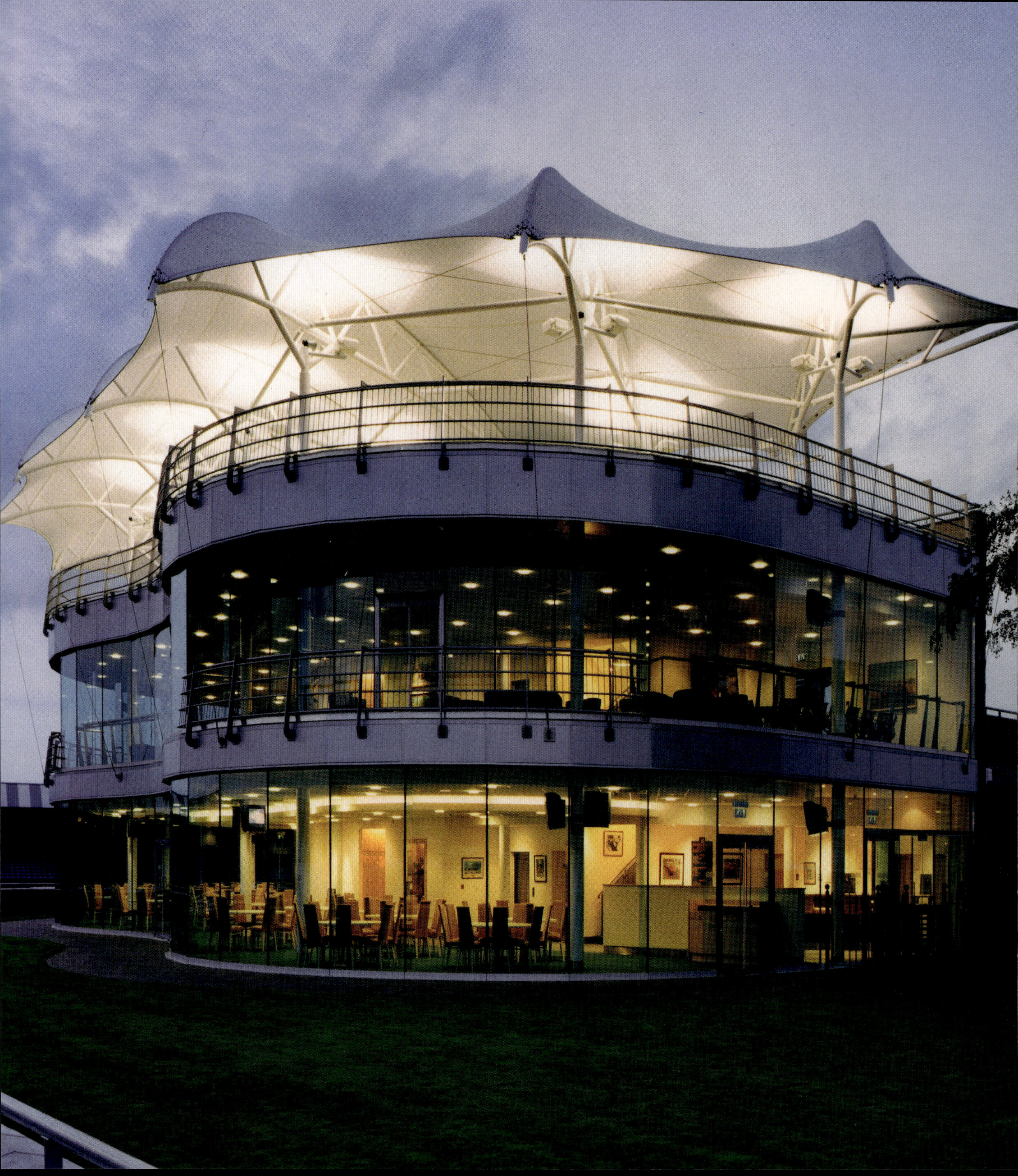

RESOURCES

For further information on any structures represented in the book, please contact the architect, engineer, or organization listed here.

Anchor Industries, Inc.
1100 Burch Drive
P.O. Box 3477
Evansville, IN 47725
www.anchorinc.com

Architen Landrell Ltd.
Station Rd., Chepstow
Monmouthshire, NP16 5PF
United Kingdom
www.architen.com

Samuel J. Armijos
89 Glenroy Road East
Fairfield, NJ 07004
www.fabricarchitect.com

Birdair
65 Lawrence Bell Drive
Amherst, NY 14221
www.birdair.com

Buro Happold
100 Broadway
New York, NY 10005
www.burohappold.com

Canobbio S.p.A
Via Roma, 3
15053 Castelnuovo Scrivia (AL)
Italy
www.canobbio.com

CENO TEC GmbH
Am Eggenkamp 14
D-48268 Greven
Germany
www.ceno-tec.de

Covertex
BahnhofstraBe 28
833119 Obing
Germany
www.covertex.com

Daroff Design Inc.
2121 Market Street
Philadelphia, PA 19103
www.daroffdesign.com

Dazian Fabrics LLC
124 Enterprise Avenue S
Secaucus, NJ 07094
www.dazian.com

DeNardis Engineering, LLC
15 Reservoir Rd.
White Plains, NY 10603
www.denardis.com

Eide Industries Inc.
16215 Piuma Avenue
Cerritos, CA 90703
www.eideindustries.com

Engineered Coated Products (ECP)
A Division of Intertape Polymer Group
50 Abbey Avenue
Truro, Nova Scotia, Canada B2N 6W4
www.intertapepolymer.com

Fabric Architecture
Unit B Nexus
Hurricane Road, Brockworth
Gloucestershire, GL3 4AG
United Kingdom
www.fabricarchitecture.com

Fabric Images Inc.
300 Corporate Drive
Elgin, IL 60123
www.fabricimages.com

Fabric Structures Inc.
184 Riverdale Rd.
Riverdale, NJ 07675
www.fabricstructuresinc.com

Fabrimax
919 S. Atlantic Blvd.
Monterey Park, CA 91754
www.fabrimax.com

Fabritec Structures
350 Kalmus Drive
Costa Mesa, CA 92626
www.fabritecstructures.com

Ferrari Textiles Corp.
1510 SW 5th Court
Pompano Beach, FL 33069
www.ferraritextiles.com

FiberTech
P.O. Box 11844
Jubail Industrial City 31961
Saudi Arabia
www.fiber-tec.com

Foiltec NA
13 Gree Mountain Drive
Cohoes, NY 12047
www.foiltecna.com

Franken Architekten GmbH
Hochstrasse 17
Frankfurt, Germany 60313
www.franken-architekten.de

FTL Design Engineering Studio
44 East 32nd Street
New York, NY 10016
www.ftlstudio.com

Geiger Engineers, PC
2 Executive Blvd., Suite 410
Suffern, NY 10901
www.geigerengineers.com

G.H. Bruce, LLC
5815 Canal Bank Road
Scottsdale, AZ 85250
www.ghbruce.com

Gisela Stromeyer Design
165 Duane Street, Suite 2B
New York, NY 10013
www.stromeyerdesign.com

Grimshaw Architects PC
100 Reade Street
New York, NY 10013
www.grimshaw-architects.com

HDO Productions
11910 Parklawn Drive
Rockville, MD 20852
www.hdotents.com

Herculite Products, Inc.
P.O. Box 435
Emigsville, PA 17318
www.herculite.com

Hightex GmbH
NordstraBe 10
83253 Rimsting
Germany
www.hightexworld.com

Industrial Fabrics Association International
1801 County Road B W
Roseville, MN 55113
www.ifai.com

Hudson Awning
27 Cottage Street
Bayonne, NJ 07002
www.hudsonawning.com

J&J Carter Ltd.
8 Lion Court
Daneshill E. Industrial Estate
Basingstoke, Hampshire RG24 8QU
United Kingdom
www.jjcarter.com

Lawrence Fabric Structures, Inc.
3509 Tree Court Industrial Blvd.
St. Louis, MO 63122
www.lawrencefabric.com

Main Attractions
85 Newfield Avenue
Edison, NJ 08837
www.mainattractions.com

MDT Inc.
Mueller Design
971 West Dogwood Trail
Tyrone, GA 30290
www.mdt-tex.com

Mehler Texnologies Inc.
175 Mehler Lane
Martinsville, VA 24112
www.mehler-texnologies.com

Miro Rivera Architects
505 Powell Street
Austin, TX 78703
www.mirorivera.com

Naizil Coated Fabrics Inc.
12667 Coleraine Dr.
P.O. Box 250
Bolton, Ontario, Canada, ON L7E 5T2
www.naizilcanada.com

P-D Interglas Technologies Ltd.
1489 Baltimore Pike, Suite 214
Springfield, PA 19064
www.atex-membranes.com

Pink Inc.
152 East 23rd Street
New York, NY 10010
www.pinkincdesign.com

Rainier Industries, Ltd.
18435 Olympic Ave. S
Seattle, WA 98188
www.rainier.net

Ronstan USA
45 Highpoint Avenue, #2
Portsmouth, RI 02871
www.ronstan.us

Rose Brand
4 Emerson Lane
Secaucus, NJ 07094
www.rosebrand.com

Saint-Gobain Performance Plastics Corp.
701 Daniel Webster Hwy.
Merrimack, NH 03054
www.sheerfill.com

Schlaich Bergermann and Partners LP
54 West 21st Street
New York, NY 10010
www.sbp.de

Seaman Corp.
100 Venture Blvd.
Wooster, OH 44691
www.seamancorp.com

Shade Structures Inc.
350 Kalmus Drive
Costa Mesa, CA 92626
www.shadestructures.net

Snyder Manufacturing
3001 Progress Street/ Box 188
Dover, OH 44622
www.snyderman.com

Sopers
P.O. Box 277
Hamilton, Ontario, Canada L8N 3E8
www.sopers.com

Span Systems Inc.
90 Pine Street
Manchester, NH 03103
www.spansystemsinc.com

Structurflex
101 Central Park Drive
Henderson
Auckland, New Zealand
www.structurflex.com

Sundance Mfg.
515 Ferguson Drive, Suite A
Orlando, FL 32805
www.sundancemfg.com

Sunmaster of Naples, Inc.
900 Industrial Blvd.
Naples, FL 34104
www.sunmasterinc.com

Sunports
8319 Chancellor Row
Dallas, TX 75247
www.sunports.com

Tensys Consultants
1 St Swithins Yard
Walcot Street
Bath BA1 5BG
United Kingdom
www.tensys.com

Tentnology Co.
15427 66th Avenue
Surrey, BC Canada V3S 2A1
www.tentnology.com

Transformit Inc.
33 Sanford Drive
Gorham, ME 04038
www.transformitdesign.com

Universal Fabric Structures
2200 Kumry Road
Quakertown, PA 18951
www.ufsinc.com

Verseidag Seemee US, Inc.
4 Aspen Road
Randolph, NJ 07869
www.seemeeus.com

Wayne Rendely, PE
132 Columbia Street
Huntington Station, NY 11746
www.waynerendelype.com

W.L. Gore & Associates Inc.
100 Airport Rd.
Elkton, MD 21921
www.gore.com/tenara

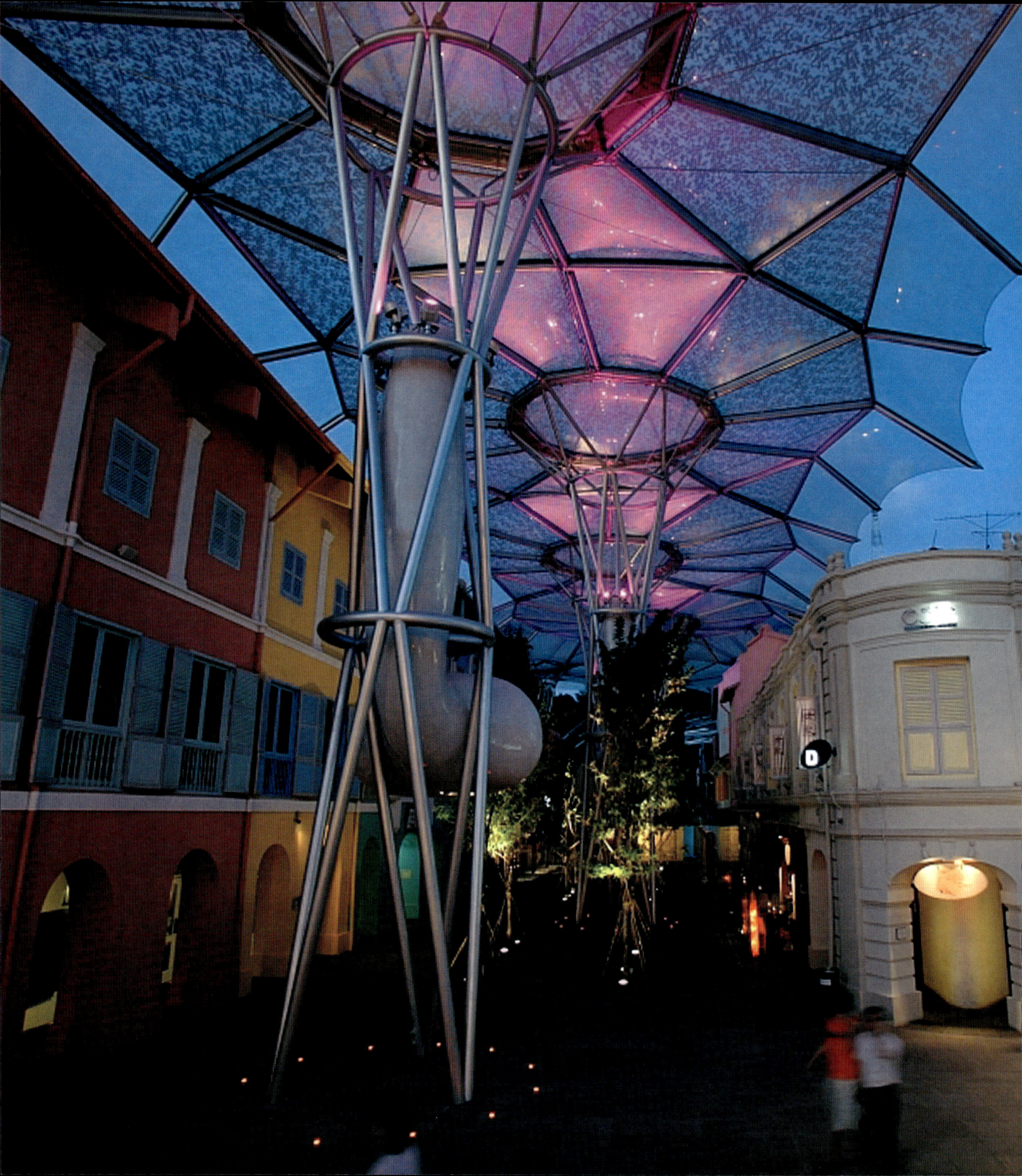

BIBLIOGRAPHY

Berger, Horst. *Light Structures: Structures of Light*, 2nd ed. Basel, Switzerland: Birkhauser, 1996.

Drew, Philip. *Tensile Architecture*. Boulder, Colorado: Westview Press, 1979.

Foster, Brian and Marijke Mollaert. *European Design Guide for Tensile Surface Structures*. TensiNet, 2004.

Ishii, Kazuo. *Membrane Structures in Japan*. Tokyo: SPS Publishing, 1995.

Koch, Klaus-Michael. *Membrane Structures*. Munich: Prestel, 2004.

Nerdinger, Winfred. *Frei Otto—Complete Works*. Basel, Switzerland: Birkhauser, 2006.

Robbin, Tony. *Engineering a New Architecture*. New Haven, Connecticut: Yale University Press, 1996.

Vandenberg, Maritz. *Soft Canopies*. London: Academy Editions, 1996.

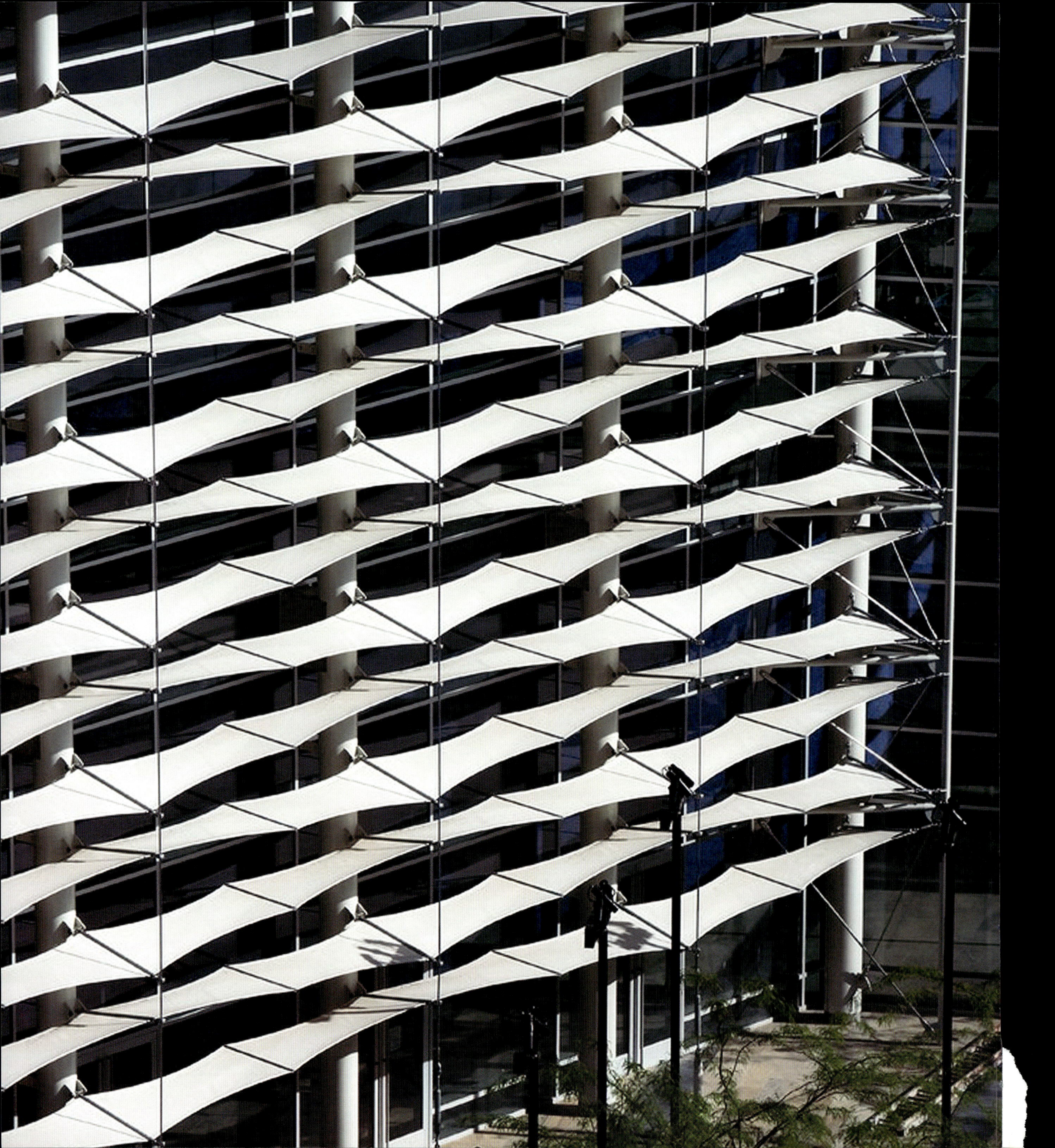

INDEX

Adams Hennon Architects, *154, 155*
Airlight, Ltd., *245–247*
Allsop Architects, *243*
Altoon Porter, *148*
American Society for Testing and Materials, 15
Anchor Industries, *97, 98, 101, 105, 109*
anticlastic surface forms, 12
Architen Landrell, *28, 61, 66, 72, 73, 75, 76, 77, 84, 85, 86, 88, 89, 94, 102, 114, 166, 172, 173, 182, 184, 185, 193, 195, 198, 206, 211, 214, 217, 227, 230, 252, 253*
arch-supported structures, 12, 181, *182–195*
Arizona
    Mesa Arts Center, *142, 159*
    Phoenix Library, *148*
    Scottsdale (Magma Ranch), *133*
    Tempe (Arizona State University), *151, 237*
Armijos, Samuel J., *21, 23, 105, 119, 170, 195, 199, 211*
Ashoken Architecture, *183*
Australia, Melbourne (Royal Melbourne Showground), *22, 157*
Austria
    Kufstein (Castle Kufstein), *17, 248–251*
    Weitra Castle, *62–64*
    Zeltweg, *228*

awnings and canopies
    definition and characteristics, 27
    examples, *28–47*

bale rings, 21, *153, 160*
Barbados, *253*
Barreiros Ferreira, *224*
barrel vault, 12, 181
base plates, 21
Base Structure, Ltd., *145*
Berger, Horst, 12
biaxial test, 14
BOORA Architects, *142*
boss plates, 21
boundaries of tensioned fabric, 12
Bruce, G. H., *125, 128, 131, 132, 138*
Will Bruder + Partners, Ltd., *148*
butt seams, 16

cabana tents, *113*
cable cuff, 13
cables, 21–22
cable strap, 13, 22
California
    American Canyon, *190*
    Burbank (Lundigan Park), *122*
    Camp Pendleton, *126*

Carlsbad (Legoland theme park), *221*
Loma Linda University, *107*
Los Angeles
    Farmers Market, *146*
    Four-Corners Retail Mall, *43*
    Palazzo resort, *44*
    12th Street Marketplace, *38*
Mission Viejo
    Kaleidoscope Mall, *148*
    Saddleback Community Church, *188*
Palm Springs Airport, *222*
Palo Alto (Mid-Peninsula Day School), *172*
Rancho Mirage
    Agua Caliente Casino, *127*
    Children's Discovery Museum, *139*
Rolling Hills Estate, *143*
Sacramento (community pool), *130*
San Diego
    Convention Center, *178*
    Mission Valley Mall, *199*
San Francisco (Collaborate office), *80, 81*
San Jose (Oakridge Mall), *132*
Santa Clara (Great America), *134*
Canada, Vancouver, *225*
Canobbio, *224, 245*
Canobbio and M. Matteo Piazza, *15, 66, 116*
Carter, J. J., *47, 55, 162, 165, 197*

263

catenaries, 12–13, 21, 22
Cenotec, 45, 67, 106, 107, 108, 109, 110, 111, 112, 165, 175, 196, 230, 231
China
    Hong Kong Yam O Railway Station, 200
    Nanjing Toll Station, 196
    Shaoxing Ke Bridge, 171
    Songjiang highway tollbooth, 233
    Tiantai (highway tollbooth), 53
clamps, 23
clear-span structures, 93
    tents, 98, 99, 100, 102, 103, 104, 105, 107
Cobre Valley High, 43
Colorado
    Boulder (Stazio complex), 170
    Denver Airport, 23
compensation factors, 14
computer-aided design, 13–14
computer patterning, 14, 16
cone structures, 12
Costa Rica, San José, 119
Covertex GmbH, 20, 59, 117, 160, 162, 187, 209, 228, 239
Croatia
    Osijek, 162

Daroff Design, 143
decompensation, 14
DeNardis Engineering, 178, 193, 222, 228
design process, 12–14
double curvature, 12
Dubai
    Burj-Al-Arab Hotel, 151
    private residence, 67
Dynamics wall and ceiling system, 70–71

Edmunds, Diana, 252
Eide Industries, 43, 44, 113
ETFE. *see* ethylenetetrafluoroethylene foil and cushions
ethylenetetrafluoroethylene foil and cushions, 19–20, 235, 239, 241
EventQuest, 236

Fabric Architecture, 18, 51, 132, 159, 161, 174
Fabric Images, 79
fabric roofs, 11

fabric structures
    applications, 11
    arch- and frame-supported structures, 181, 182–211
    awnings and canopies, 27, 28–47
    components, 20–23
    definition, 11
    design process, 12–14
    future prospects, 235
    historical development, 11
    interior applications, 69, 70–92
    mast-supported, 152, 154–179
    point-supported structures, 212, 213, 214–233
    shade structures, 121, 122–139
    temporary structures, 93, 94–120
    tension in, 12
    textile façades, 140, 141, 142–151
    umbrellas, 49, 50–67
Fabrimax, 53, 164, 171, 230, 233
Fabritec Structures, 10, 12, 18, 20, 21, 23, 33, 34, 35, 36, 38, 39, 43, 44, 50, 52, 56, 61, 65, 91, 107, 132, 134, 138, 139, 146, 147, 148, 154, 155, 160, 162, 164, 172, 174, 183, 188, 190, 199, 201, 202, 209, 214, 217, 218, 219, 221, 241, 251, 253
façades, textile, 140, 141, 142–151
fan vaults, 181
Ferrari Textiles, 38, 57, 76, 77, 80, 143, 144, 145, 186, 190, 204, 205
fiberglass
    polytetrafluoroethylene-coated, 17
    silicone-coated, 17
Fibertech, 65, 164, 165, 167, 168, 183, 187, 196, 200, 215, 229
fill, 14
fire resistance, 15
Florida
    Boca Raton (Florida Atlantic University), 35
    Naples
        Arthrex office, 30
        Caribe and Cove Towers, 42
        Esplanade awning, 41
        Horsecreek carport, 36
        Le Rivage Condominium, 37, 40
        Main Street awnings, 28
        Martin House, 39

        Navona condominium, 130
        Port Royal Club, 42
        Provence Condominiums, 30, 33
    Orlando
        Cirque de Soleil building, 226
        International Airport, 36
        Sea World, 21
    West Palm Beach (City Place Project), 28
flying masts, 21, 100, 101
form-finding, 13–14
frame-supported structures, 12, 196–211
    applications, 181
    design characteristics, 181
frame tents, 93, 97, 101, 107, 109
France
    Banque Populaire de L'Atlantique, 80
    Lille (Halles de Wazemmes), 77
    Lyon (Gerland Stadium), 186
    Marie d'Antony, 76
    Valenton, 204, 205
Franken Architecture, 147
FTL Design Engineering Studio, 13, 16, 19, 38, 56, 59, 95, 96, 115, 118, 119, 142, 148, 159, 170, 171, 179, 185, 200, 223, 226, 236, 237, 247, 251, 252, 254

Geiger Engineers, 166, 167, 177, 221, 225
Georgia, Atlanta (Olympic Village), 118, 200
Germany
    Berlin (Olympic Stadium), 194
    Chiemsee (Prienavera Pool), 240
    Frankfurt
        BMW, 147, 239
        Papageno Children's Theatre, 209
    Gersthofen TSV Grandstand, 175
    Hamburg, Medienbunker, 106
    Hanover Stadium, 20
    Leipzig Airport, 230, 231
    Mainau, 196
    Monschau Castle, 108
    Munich
        Froettmaning U-Bahn Station, 187
        HVB Bank, 238
    Potsdam, 65
    Straubing, Founders' Center, 45
    Stuttgart (VFB Club), 216

Warnemuen (Passenger Ferry Terminal), *160*
Wurzburg Chamber of Commerce, *59*
Gore, *17, 62–64, 238, 248–251*
green design, *235*
Nicholas Grimshaw and Partners, *244*
GSB Architects, *174*

hardware, 21–23, *23*
HDO, *94, 95, 112*
HDPE. see polyethylene, high-density
Heikkinen-Komonen Architects, *223*
Richard Hemingway & Partners, *184*
Adams Hennon Architects, *10, 18*
Herron, Ron, *172*
high-point curvature, *12*
Hightexworld, *150, 151, 188, 189, 194, 208, 216, 223, 239, 240, 241, 243, 244, 255*
Hillier, *91*
historical development of fabric structures, *11*
Hopkins Architects, *114, 172, 217, 223, 239*
Horst Berger Partners, *228*
House & Robertson, *146*
Huntsman AG, *80, 81*
hypar structures, *12, 55, 213*
    shade structures, *125, 129*

Illinois
    DeKalb (Northern Illinois University), *35*
    St. Charles Youth Park, *36*
interior fabric structures, *70–92*
    applications, *69*
    fabric qualities, *69*
Iowa, Cedar Falls (University of Northern Iowa), *193*
Ireland, Cork, *197*
Italy
    Milan (Piazza Italia), *224*
    Venafro (Chemical Research Centre), *15*

Japan, Nansei yacht club, *241*

Kapoor, Anish, *255*
Keder edge, *22*
Kentucky, Louisville Park, *52*
Koch, Klaus-Michael, *12*
Korea, Seoul, World Cup Stadium, *166*
Kuwait Airport, *167*

lacing, *27*
lap seams, *16*
Lawrence Fabric Structures, *36, 40, 44*
Leadership in Energy and Environmental Design, *235*
LightHouseOne, *189*
load analysis, *14*
low-point curvature, *12*
Luxenbourg, Kirchberg, *165*

Main Attractions, *96, 97, 101, 103, 104, 109*
Maryland
    Baltimore (Pier 6 Music Pavilion), *170*
    Gaithersburg (Arbee Associates), *38*
Massachusetts, Boston (Top of the Hub Restaurant), *70*
mast-supported structures, *12, 152, 153, 154–179*
    components, *21*
    definition and design characteristics, *153*
materials
    arch-supported structures, *181*
    fabric selection, *15, 20*
    for interior applications, *69*
    membrane fabrication, *16*
    samples, *20*
    types of, *11, 14–15, 16–20*
MDT-TEX, *50, 55, 57, 61*
membrane
    definition, *16*
    fabrication, *16*
membrane plates, *12, 21, 153, 217*
Mexico, Puebla (Auchan Food Court), *208*
Michigan
    Detroit (Rosa Parks Bus Station), *237*
    Kent (Millennium Park), *221*
Minnesota, Prior Lake (Mystic Lake Casino), *50*
Miro Rivera Architects, *135, 226*
Missouri
    Kansas City (18th and Vine Pavilion), *23, 214*
    St. Louis
        Children's Hospital, *44*
        Vindeset, *40*
modeling, *13–14*
Montana, Missoula (Carras Park), *178*
Carlos Mosely Music Pavilion, *115*

Naizil, *111, 224*
National Fire Protection Association, *15*
Navitrac tent system, *98*
Nevada
    Las Vegas
        Caesars Palace, *39, 174*
        Centennial Hills Park, *122*
        Darling Tennis Center, *124*
        Executive Airport, *202*
        MGM Convention Center, *199*
        Motor Speedway, *201*
        Premium Outlet Mall, *10, 18, 20, 21, 154, 155, 217*
New Jersey
    Edgewater Ferry Terminal, *44*
    Flemington auto dealership, *65*
    Princeton University, *91, 195, 199*
    Weehawken (Port Imperial Ferry Terminal), *202, 203*
New York
    Annandale-on-Hudson (Bard College), *183*
    New York City
        Bryant Park Ice Rink, *105*
        Central Park summer stage, *115*
        Cooper Hewitt Museum, *251*
        Elie Tahari fashion event, *83*
        Equinox Pool, *78*
        Hammerstein Ballroom, *91*
        Hudson River Park, *160*
        John F. Kennedy Airport, *44*
        Roth residence, *83*
        World Financial Center Winter Garden, *19*
    Pawling (Cogi Farms), *61, 162*
    Staten Island, *56*
    White Plains (Nokia), *218, 219*
New Zealand
    Auckland, *191*
        airport, *143*
        Fullers Ferry, *34*
        Netball complex, *201*
        Tennis Centre, *204*
    Challenge petrol stations, *175*
    Great Barrier Island (Noble House), *184*
    Waiheke Island, Matiatia Wharf, *210*
    Wellington
        Hutt International Boys School, *232, 233*
        Porirua Mall, *22, 168*

North Carolina
    Charlotte Bandshell, *211*
    Raleigh-Durham, *221*
    Winston-Salem (Sara Lee headquarters), *56*
Norway, Kongsberg, Tubaloon Performance Shelter, *245*

Ohio, Cleveland (Nautica Amphitheater), *177*
Oklahoma, Tulsa Airport, *190*
Oregon, Oswego, *214*
Otto, Frei, 11, 12

PD Interglas, *16, 245–247*
Pennsylvania
    Philadephia
        Philadephia Park, *143*
        Trilogy Apartments, *33*
    Pittsburgh (Carnegie Science Center), *59*
perimeter masts, 21, 153
photovoltaic thin-film technology, 235, *251*
Pink Inc., *72, 78, 85, 91*
pneumatic structures, 235, 236
Point Defiance Zoo, *33*
point-supported structures, 12, *212, 214–233*
    definition and design characteristics, 213
pole tents, 93, *111*
polyester
    PVC-coated, 18
    PVC-laminated, 18
polyethylene, high-density, 19
polytetrafluoroethylene, woven, 17–18
polytetrafluoroethylene-coated fiberglass, 17
polyvinylchloride. *see* polyester, PVC-coated; polyester, PVC-laminated
polyvinyl fluoride, 18
polyvinylidene fluoride, 18
Portugal
    Guarda, *108*
    Lisbon (Expo98), *66, 224*
positive curvature, 12
PTFE. *see* polytetrafluoroethylene, woven; polytetrafluoroethylene-coated fiberglass

radial cable, 21
radio-frequency welding, 18
Rainier Industries, *33, 110, 144, 146, 151, 178*
reflectivity, 15

reinforcement, 16
ridge cables, 21, 213
Rockwell Group, *226*
Richard Rogers Partnership Architects, *166*
roped edge, 22

Salgado, *66*
Samyn and Partners, *15*
Saudi Arabia
    Dammam
        Al Shatee Mall, *215*
        Marina Mall, *229*
    Riyadh
        Al Hamra Oasis Sports Center, *168*
        Carrefour Shopping Mall, *187*
        Fahd Stadium, *167*
Sbriglio/Multipack, *116*
Scotland, Glasgow Fort Shopping Park, *16*
seams, 16
shackles, 23
Shade Structures, *122, 126, 130, 133, 134, 136*
shade structures, 122–139
    applications, 121
    design characterstics, 121
silicone-coated fiberglass, 17
Singapore
    Clarke Quay shopping mall, *243*
    United World College, *23, 206*
SNØHETTA, *245*
space frame, 181
Spain, Madrid (Xanadu shopping mall), *183*
spandex, 19
stretch fabrics, 19
Gisela Stromeyer Architectural Design, *72, 78, 80, 81, 83, 86, 87, 89, 90*
structural analysis, 14
Structurflex, *22, 23, 34, 143, 157, 158, 168, 175, 184, 191, 201, 202, 203, 204, 206, 210, 216, 232, 233*
Sunmaster of Naples, *28, 30, 33, 36, 37, 39, 40, 41, 42, 130*
Sunports, *52, 55, 56, 122, 123, 124, 126, 127, 128, 129, 131, 132, 133, 134, 135, 136, 137, 139, 146, 147, 148, 154, 155, 160, 162, 164, 172, 174, 176, 183, 188, 190, 199, 201, 202, 214, 217, 218, 219, 221, 241, 251, 253*

Switzerland
    Bulle (Yendi Building), *144*
    Lausanne, *150*
    Montreaux, *245–247*
    Neuchatel (Expo 2002), *116*
    Suhr (Migros Distribution Center), *145*
    Zurich (Incognito Club), *86*
synclastic surface forms, 12

teepee, *110*
temporary structures and tents, 93, *94–120*
    definitions and characteristics, 93
    materials, 18
Tensairity, *245–247*
tensile membrane structures, 11
tension
    boundaries, 12
    catenaries, 12–13
    forms of fabric structures, 12
tension tents, 93, *109, 112*
Tensys, *14, 252*
Tentnology, *100, 101, 102*
tents. *see* temporary structures and tents
Texas
    Allen, Celebration Park, *176*
    Dallas
        Bahama Beach, *56*
        Executive Airport, *52*
        Love Field, *209*
        Zoo, *128*
    Desoto (Grimes Park), *131*
    Grand Prairie (McFalls Park), *133*
    Grapevine, *124*
    Harlington (HEB Supermarket), *164*
    Lake Austin, *226*
    Pearland (Southdown Park), *126*
    Woodlands (Cynthia Woods Mitchell Center), *228*
textile buildings, 11
Thailand, Bangkok Airport, *188*
theatrical draperies, 19
tiedown cables, 21, 22
Transformit, *19, 70, 71, 73, 74, 79, 80, 90, 91*
transmission, 15
turnbuckles, 23

umbrellas
    butterfly, *61*
    definition and characteristics, *49*
    examples, *50–67*
    inverted, *49, 56, 57, 65*
    retractable, *62–64*
    sidearm, *65*
    Type E inverted, *50*
    Type T, *55*
United Arab Emirates, *151*
    Abu Dhabi Corniche, *158*
    Al Ain (VMF Market), *216*
United Kingdom, *132*
    Alnwick Garden, *239*
    Andover (Lights–Cricklade College Theater), *47*
    Apple HQ, *28*
    Ascot Racecourse, *208*
    Ashford (Outlet Village Retail), *166*
    Bisley, *164*
    Bristol
        Cotham School, *227*
        Cribbs Causeway, *184*
        Elmlea School, *102*
    Cosford (RAF Museum), *145*
    Edmonton Green Station, *195*
    Essex (auto dealership), *51*
    Gloucester (Kingswalk Shopping Centre), *73*
    Glyndebourne Opera House, *172*
    Kent (Chatham Maritime), *185*
    Leicester (National Space Centre), *244*
    Liverpool (Chandlers Wharf), *159*
    London
        BBC Bandshell, *85, 252*
        British Museum, *77*
        Buckingham Palace temporary structure, *114*
        Imagination Building, *172*
        Kingly Court, *61*
        Millenium Dome, *94*
        O2 Riverwalk, *75, 198*
        Plashet Unity Bridge, *193*
        Quayside Housing Development, *174*
        Reuters Building, *76*
        Stratford bus interchange, *66*
        Tate Modern, *255*
        Longton (Thomas Moore College Pavilion), *18, 161*
    Murton (Dalton Park Shopping Mall), *173*
    Newbury (Vodafone building), *230*
    Nottingham (Inland Revenue Centre), *223*
    Oxford, *252*
    Plymouth (Sainsbury's Marsh Mills Superstore), *206*
    Silverstone, British Racing Drivers Club, *211*
    Southampton (Hampshire Rose Bowl), *217*
    Surrey (Sandown Park Racecourse), *55*
    Whitehaven Pavilion, *165*
    Woolwich (Queen Elizabeth Hospital), *214*
Universal Fabric Structures, *99, 102*
Utah, Salt Lake City (Winter Olympics), *146*

valley cables, *22, 213*
Virginia
    Ballston, *34*
    Charlottesville Amphitheater, *185*
    Hampton Roads Convention Center, *16, 171, 179*

Wakely, David, *80, 81*
warp, *14*
Washington, DC
    Embassy of Finland, *223*
    Holiday Inn, *147*
    National Symphony Orchestra bandstand, *119*
Washington, Tacoma, Cheney Stadium, *144*
WDG Architecture, *147*
WS Atkins Architects, *151*

X-Ten Architecture, *143*

yurt, *110*

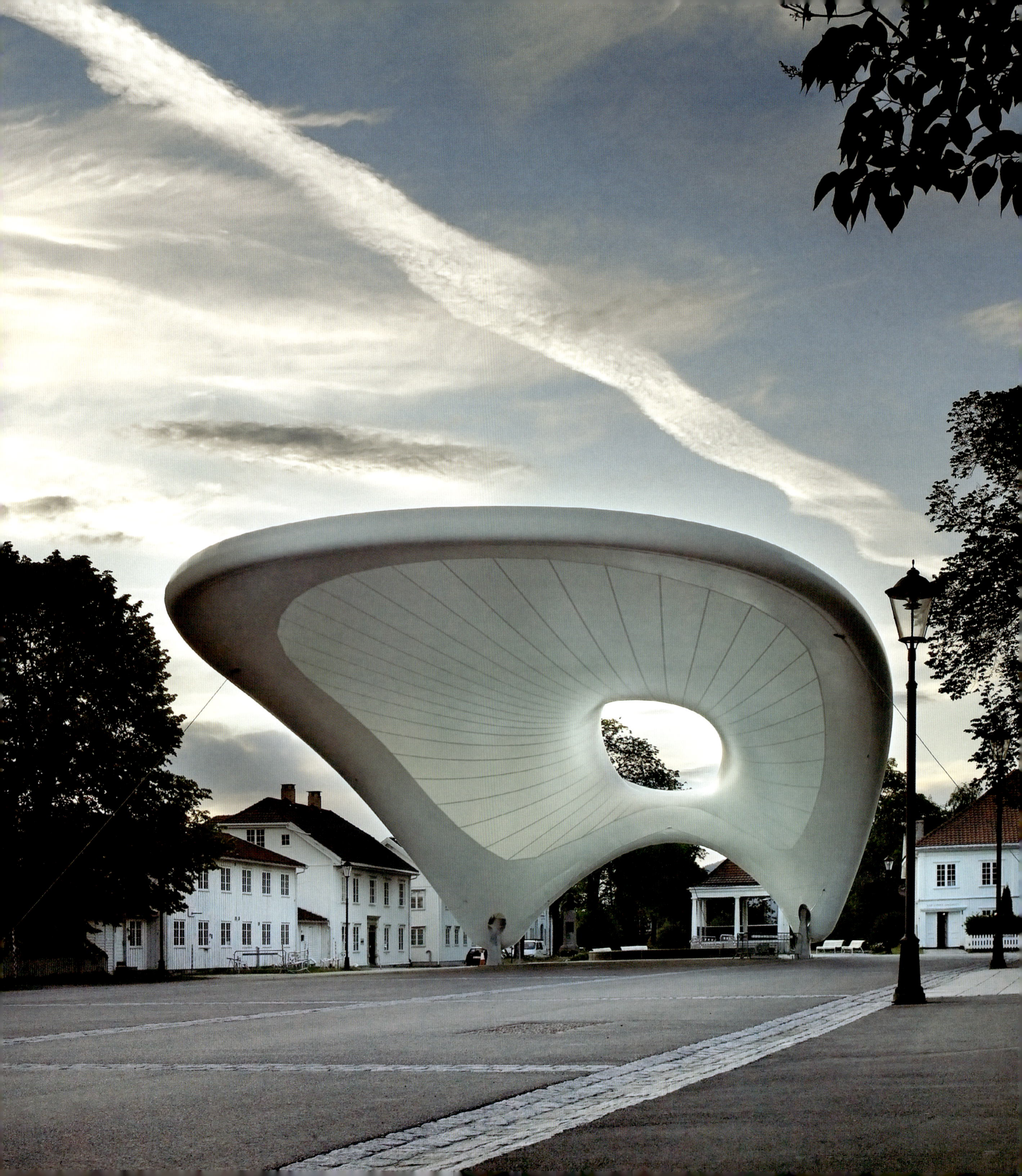

ABOUT THE SAMPLES

When it comes to fabric structures, it is very common to get fabric samples. Fabric comes in different weights, translucencies, and textures, among other characteristics, and it helps to touch and feel the *exact* material so there is no misunderstanding among clients, designers, and fabricators. Samples should be submitted to the client and a sign-off or approval is highly recommended. The samples provided in this book include: an unbleached Teflon-coated fiberglass (Saint Gobain) which, when exposed to the sun, will turn white; and two highly translucent white fabrics made of woven PTFE (Tenara by Gore) and silicone-coated fiberglass (Atex), which are more pliable than standard PTFE. Vinyl-coated polyester (Ferrari Textile) comes in a variety of weights and topcoats: one sample is the most commonly used 1002T2, which has a high-gloss finish; the other is Façades Textile 371, which is used for both vertical and horizontal shading applications. The high-density polyethylene (Multiknit), the most economical of the samples, serves for shading and light water protection.

Special thanks go to the manufacturers who provided samples for the book. Complete contact information for them can be found in the Resources section.

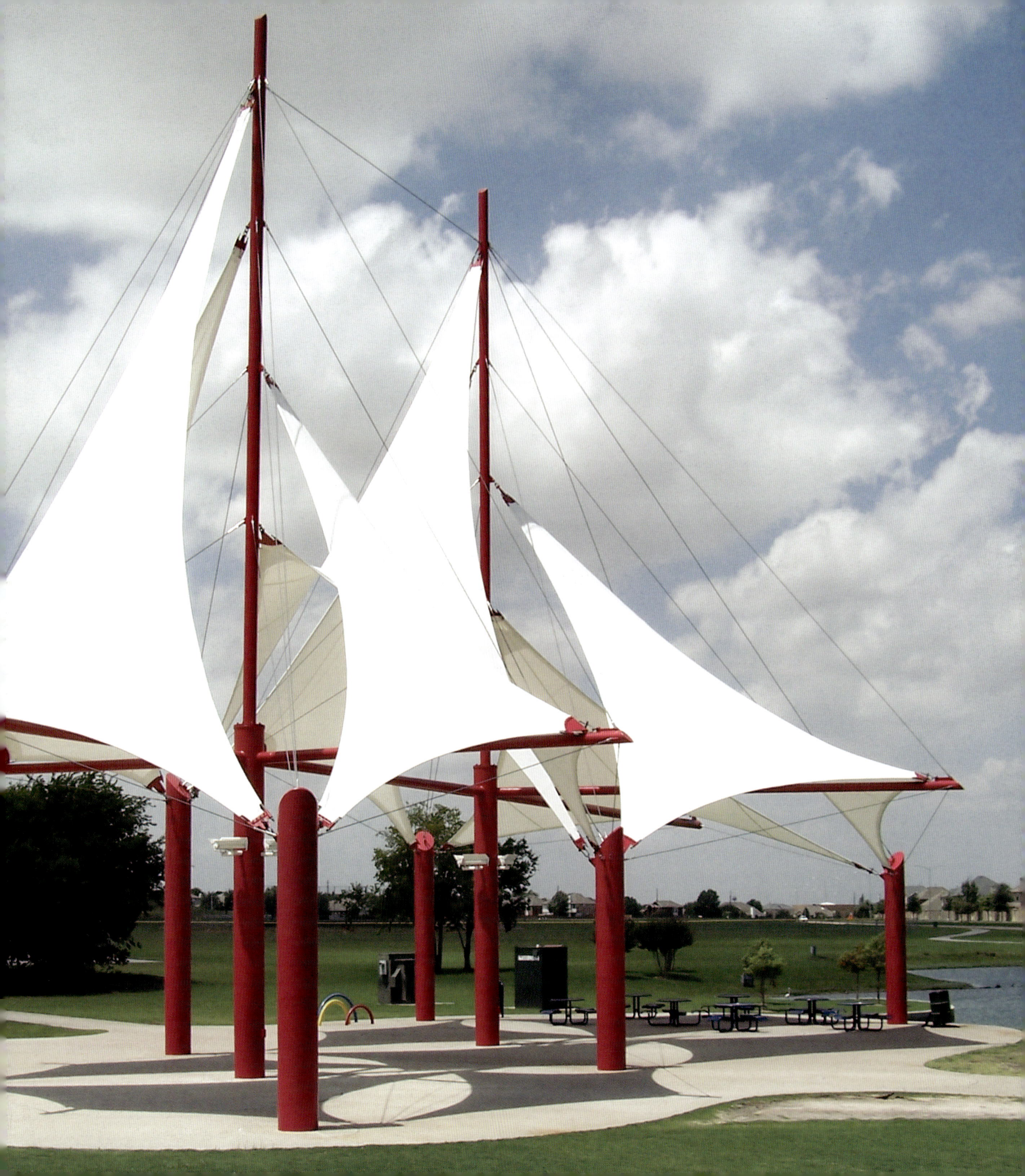

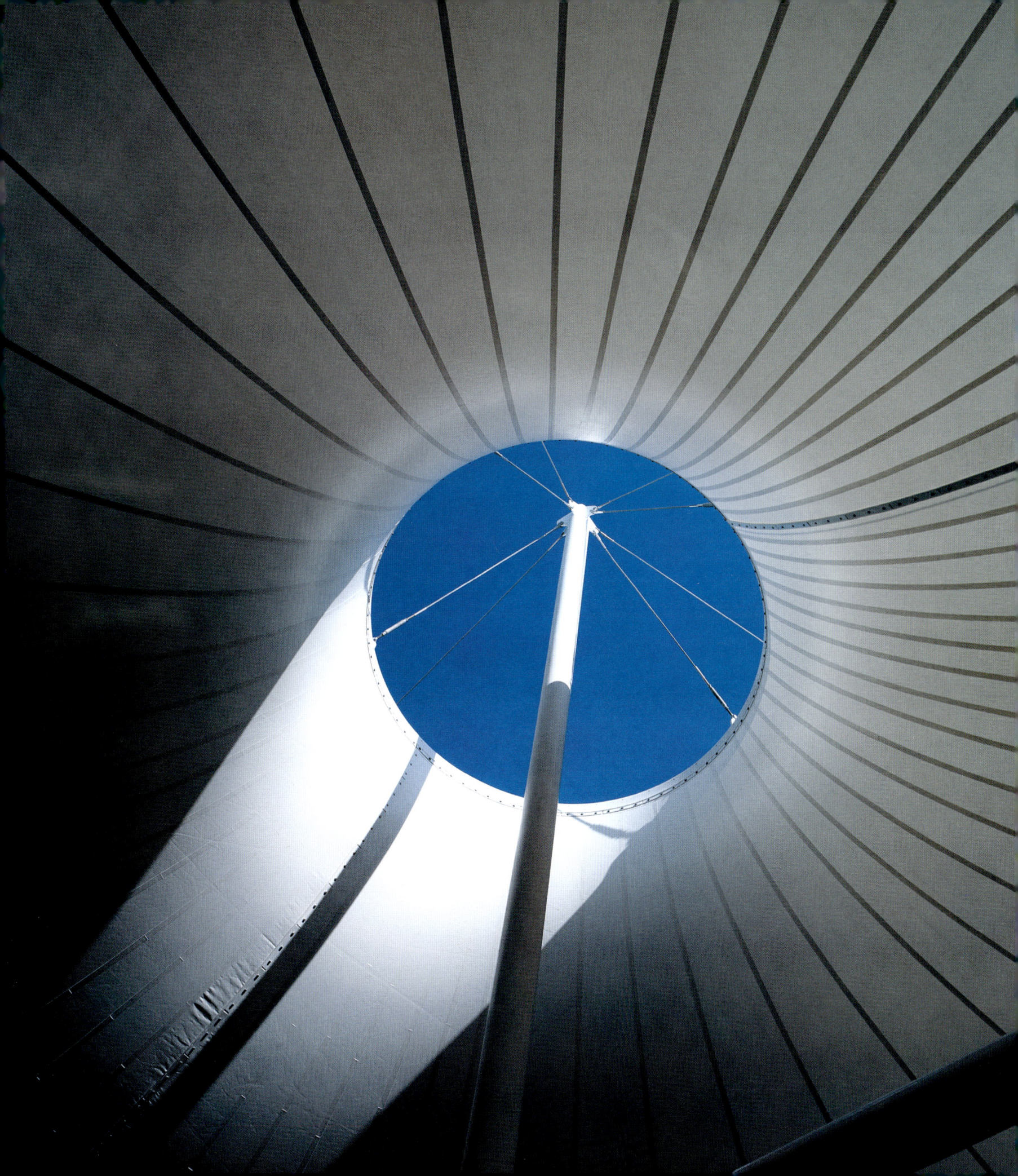